# Musical Hugs

## Succeeding through Serving, One Song at a Time

Jacob,
"Musical Hugs" To you!

### By Larry V. Dykstra

Inspire On Purpose Publishing

Irving, Texas

# Acknowledgments

I always expected to write a book one day, just not this one. The book I had in mind was an impersonal treatment of a technical area of expertise I'd garnered during my career, not the story of the personal journey that ensued.

It was during discussions with Kent Potter and Rita Bailey regarding a separate book project that the idea for this work surfaced. "You should tell your story first," said Rita, and the seed was planted.

I resisted the idea for weeks, torn between concern that my ego wasn't strong enough to see me through the project and a fear that others would consider my ego too large should I complete the book. But Rita coached me to embrace sharing my experiences so that others could learn from them. It is my sincere hope that this book delivers on that intention.

Because I could not have done this alone, I have many individuals to thank:

Jim Newton, the founder of Hugworks, who has been playing his guitar and singing in children's hospitals for over thirty years. Jim was willing to share his tremendous breadth and depth of knowledge. If my story is about discovering the value of selflessly serving others, Jim's dedication provided the perfect example.

Dr. Robert Krout, Paul G. Hill, and Judith Ritchie, mentors, who in ways unique to each of them revealed to me the helpful and healing power of music across diverse audiences and settings.

Carmen Goldthwaite, my instructor, who patiently repeated lessons I was slow to adopt. Early on she advised me to include personal experiences in my writing. "You are part of the story," she suggested. Sage advice from a sage.

Michelle Morse, my publisher, who kept this project on track. She artfully balanced pushing me forward when I felt tempted to slow down, while providing the time and space to allow the ideas behind my words to incubate.

Rebecca Chown, my editor, who embraced the subject and brought life, organization, and clarity to early drafts. I was blessed by her positive spirit of encouragement that gave me the confidence I needed.

My parents, whose long lives offer a positive example of a strong marriage, enduring faith, and the character building that comes from hard work. I feel blessed and favored to be able to call them "Mom and Dad."

Finally, my wife Sandy for her encouragement and support of this effort and my many other pursuits. Because of her expertise as a teacher of English as a Second Language, I have the luxury of my own style manual readily available. Acquaintances who have had the chance to meet Sandy think better of me as a result. I know what love feels like each time I see her across a crowded room.

# Dedication

This book is dedicated to the millions of children who spend too much precious time in hospitals each year. The strength and grace I have seen them demonstrate in the face of life challenges both inspires and humbles me.

I also dedicate this work to those who support these children: the parents, siblings, grandparents, doctors, nurses, child life specialists, and volunteers. The list is endless, like the devotion they displayed through their caring for "the least of these."

# Disclaimer

The stories recorded here are based on actual events I experienced with real patients and families. The names and identifying details of all these individuals have been modified or omitted to protect their privacy and ensure confidentiality. In addition, the names of the hospitals in which I volunteered have been omitted to avoid any perception that I am speaking on their behalf.

With their permission, I have retained the names of a few individuals whose insight and expertise helped me along my journey. I am grateful to be able to acknowledge the unselfish support and service Jim Newton, Paul G. Hill, Judith Ritchie, and Dr. Robert Krout provide to others each day. Jim and Paul also granted their permission to reprint lyrics to original Hugworks songs they composed and to which they hold the rights. I am thankful for their generosity.

# Table of Contents

# Introduction
## The Song Is the Tree

There is nearly universal agreement about the ability of music to access humanity's deepest emotions. We know this innately. We cry, smile, and tap our feet to the pulse of the sounds we hear. A song comes on the radio, and we are transported to a meaningful place and time unavailable to us only moments before. What else in our lives has the power to be so evocative?

Songs, or parts of them, get stuck in our heads and won't go away. Through them, we experience and engage in music, discuss music, and purchase, play, and request music. We want songs, and we ask for them by name. If the forest is music, its components – melody, tempo, rhythm, venue – are like the bark or leaves. The song itself? Well, the song is the tree.

I have been fortunate to lead many group sing-alongs in my lifetime, and I've never heard anyone say, "Larry, play something in the key of G that contains lyrics that express a sense of longing that is supported by a closing, soaring lead-guitar solo."

Instead, people shout, "Play 'Free Bird'!"

Nearly everyone knows what that title means. They hear the music when the title is spoken. Inevitably, they recall a time when they heard this song played.

I doubt I would have given this topic much thought if a friend hadn't approached me some years ago with a question I'd never before considered. Richard, a graphic artist who creates beautiful paintings as his hobby, gave me two prints for my birthday that hang in my cozy home office. Several weeks before he gave them to me, I performed a song at a local church event. I'd taken a poem written in honor of a recently deceased matriarch and arranged it into a musical piece. I was proud of the composition, my performance, and the audience's response, but then…

"Larry," Richard said, "I'm not sure I understand why you do it."

"What do you mean?" I asked.

"The song you did the other night. I could tell you put a lot of work into it. And I liked it. But once it was over, you had nothing to show for your effort. It's lost forever."

"I'd never really thought of it that way," I said.

The truth was, I'd never given much thought at all to why I sing for others or myself. It's just something I've enjoyed doing since I was ten years old. Wasn't that enough?

Richard continued, "As a graphic artist, after I spend hours working on a piece, bringing it to life, fine-tuning it, I have something I can look at and admire. There's a physical reminder of what I've accomplished. But you can't do that with a song. Once you've performed it, there's nothing left. So I don't understand why you do it."

Richard's remarks raised some fundamental questions. Why did I sing, and did songs really matter?

These questions bothered me for months. By "bothered," I mean something like a dull, nagging toothache that wouldn't completely go away but was never troublesome enough to address. But one day, in October of 2009, I sang a song to a hospitalized teenager named Jason and caught a glimpse of an answer to Richard's inquiry. I discovered the inherent power in a single song. That experience gave me a reason to sing and a new audience to sing to – severely ill children and their families.

Playing a single song to one patient also set me on a personal journey that opened in me a new understanding of what "success" means. By going into the hospital rooms of severely ill children and offering them music, I discovered what "serving" looks and feels like. My reward came in the form of defining myself more by what I do for others than by what I do for a living.

This book is a collection of short stories recounting individual hospital visits that reveal the power of music as a healing force. This work also chronicles significant music and life lessons

I learned during my journey. My hope is that these firsthand accounts will demonstrate how live music presented to severely ill children and their caregivers has the power to bring comfort and healing "one song at a time."

# Part One
## My Journey into the Healing Power of a Single Song

After five years and hundreds of visits, today I succeeded at signing in at the hospital without peeking at the number printed on the back of my volunteer badge. This may be a minor achievement, but to me it's worth noting. Most of my thirty-year career involved research and analysis, yet somehow I was never very good at remembering figures.

Lyrics to songs were never a problem, but numbers? Count me out.

In the hospital, my aptitude at lyric recall comes in handy. For the next hour or so, I will walk the inpatient floors providing songs for severely ill children and their caregivers without the aid of printed music. Having my repertoire committed to memory allows me to completely focus on how my audience is responding and to make any adjustments that might be needed. Here I must be single-mindedly attentive to the needs of others, but I wasn't always this way.

I am among the hundreds of volunteers regularly donating my time and skills at this large metropolitan hospital. Everyone has their personal reasons for being here, although we don't often share them with each other. Regardless of our motivation, we are aligned around a common purpose: to make the stays of hospitalized children as positive as possible.

My guitar case draws the attention of visitors and staff alike. It certainly gets noticed at the office where the volunteers gather, in part because I can never seem to avoid banging it into the door as I enter.

"Good morning," I say with a smile to the woman sitting behind the desk at the computer dedicated to volunteer sign-in. In her masterful portrayal of indifference I have grown accustomed to, she barely acknowledges my presence. I wonder if she is irritated by my clumsy entrance, but I doubt that. I imagine her to be a good and nice person, though none of her warmth or kindness seems directed at me. I laugh inside, wondering if she will ever return my smile. Maybe next week.

Her detached response to my greeting serves as a helpful reminder of the importance of first impressions. I will meet more people in the next hour than I might have encountered in a month during my working years. I will knock on doors and ask if some music would be helpful. I am a stranger offering an unexpected service in a unique environment under unusual circumstances. The decision to accept or reject my offer may hinge more on how I present myself than on how a given patient may feel at the moment. I must do my best to be fully present and positive when I enter each room and greet whoever is inside.

Outside its case, my guitar brightens my disposition as it meets the open air. It has been a loyal companion for almost thirty years. A Guild dreadnought, it was the most expensive guitar I felt I could afford at the time I purchased it. The company isn't as well known or as popular as Martin or Taylor, but the guitar players I meet seem to know and appreciate the name.

Today, my Guild shows its age. The scratches, dings, and worn finish offer testimony of hours of practice, sing-along sessions, and time on stage. A two-inch-long crack just below the pick guard on the spruce soundboard is merely a cosmetic problem, but the crack that appeared a couple of years ago where the neck meets the headstock (and the tension of the strings is extremely high) was truly life threatening.

The scar from the repair is only noticeable to others if I care to point it out, but I am always aware of the damage done and dread the possibility that the problem may someday return. The children here may think about their health challenges in an oddly similar way, hopefully healed for the moment but never able to fully stop worrying about if or when their disease might reappear.

Like the taste of a fine wine, my Guild's voice has improved and become more distinct with age. As I adjust the tuning, I can feel it come alive, pleading to be heard. It roars when I strum it, projecting deep tones into this small space. I make a mental note to throttle back when I visit patient rooms and avoid striking its six strings too aggressively lest the sound overpower my delicate audience.

The volunteer gathering room is a small space with lockers on one end, volunteer smocks and vests hanging on the opposite wall, and a small table in the middle covered with goodies to be delivered to the children.

"Is that a Guild?" asks an older gentleman sitting at the table wearing his royal blue volunteer vest.

"Yes, it is. Do you play?"

"No, not the guitar," he replies. "I used to play French horn with the Chicago Symphony, but I was forced to quit a couple years ago when I developed health issues."

"Oh, I am so sorry," I say.

We spend the next few minutes exploring his lengthy career as a professional musician. Our conversation shifts to an unsuccessful attempt to connect our Chicago experiences by comparing the time periods we lived there and names of people and places we each knew. "It is a big city," I conclude, ending our fruitless search to find a common past.

"What did you do for a living before you became a volunteer?" the man asks in a reciprocal gesture, no doubt sensing it polite to ask me about my career since he was given the opportunity to share a bit of his own.

"I worked in business," I respond. "But that was awhile ago and not very important anymore."

He appears to recognize my answer for what I sincerely hope it is – a polite, satisfactory response that offers few details and invites no follow-up queries.

"It's too bad about having to give up the French horn," I say. "Have you ever thought about playing another instrument like the guitar?" I attempt to move the conversation back toward common ground.

"No. I may be too old for that," he says.

I consider challenging his view. Many friends have shared with me their budding interest in learning to play. I always tell them, "It's easy to learn but impossible to master." I now worry this might be more discouraging than encouraging since, to my knowledge, none of them has ever taken up the instrument.

I continue the slow tuning process. The pitch of individual strings swing toward either sharp or flat due to temperature changes, causing wooden instruments like this one to go out of tune quickly.

"So what do you do here at the hospital?" the man asks, interrupting my concentration and tuning process with a new line of questioning. "I've been a volunteer for quite a while, and I've never seen a guitar here before."

I'm not certain how best to explain it. A technical description might suffice, but I fear that for a classically trained musician who has likely forgotten more about music than I ever learned, it will fail to capture the essence of what I do. I offer a simple mental image instead. "I provide musical hugs."

"What is a musical hug?" he asks.

"Well, you've spent some time here so I imagine you understand that the kids are going through a lot physically and emotionally."

"For sure," he nods.

"They need love and support, but medical equipment, painful areas, or infectious disease guidelines can limit physical contact, making it impractical to hold, much less hug, them. I'm here to provide 'musical hugs' – expressions of love and caring in the form of live music, one song at a time."

"Interesting," he says. "How did you get into providing that kind of service?"

"That's a pretty long story," I reply, hoping to remain in the present moment rather than delve into the past.

"I have the time," he says.

So I begin sharing with him my journey into the healing power of a single song.

# Chapter One
## "Plutoed" toward a New World

The year 2006 marked the beginning of my twelfth year as a vice president of consumer insights and innovation at a Fortune 500 company, preceded by more than ten years working on national powerhouse brands like Kraft and Gatorade.

My first inkling of trouble on the horizon came during my annual performance review. My supervisor told me, "I gave you a positive review, Larry. I'm not sure if that's going to be good or bad for you."

Within a week of delivering these cryptic words, he was gone. I was left with a new boss and a mysterious dark cloud hanging over my head. Our business results were generally positive. They'd weakened a bit of late, but the future still looked promising. Nonetheless, within six months, my responsibilities had been cut in half.

I wasn't alone. Around this same time, the International Astronomic Association voted that Pluto no longer met the definition of a planet. Apparently, to be designated a planet you have to demonstrate your importance by clearing your neighborhood of other minor objects like asteroids. Pluto hadn't shown the ability to be untouchable, and neither had I.

Amidst the public outcry over Pluto's demotion, a new verb was introduced into the English language. "To pluto" came to mean "to demote or devalue someone or something." The word became so popular that the American Dialect Society declared "plutoed" its 2006 word of the year. How appropriate, as it perfectly described what was happening to me and countless other business professionals before me.

Late in 2007, I agreed to stay on for another year to help train my replacement to lead our innovation efforts. I liked the idea of teaching others, of giving something back as my career reached its close.

Meanwhile, I began to look forward to an early retirement. I wasn't certain what I would do, but I did know one thing – I wanted to keep using my music to help others because I knew firsthand how powerfully it could bind human beings together.

Years earlier, I'd brought my guitar to an off-site meeting with our executive team after someone had suggested a late night sing-along might be nice. This was right up my alley, as I'd long ago learned to play the twenty or so songs most adults know and can be enticed to sing, songs like "Brown-Eyed Girl," "Margaritaville," "Stand By Me," "Under the Boardwalk," and the like.

Leading a group on that last number has always been a personal joy. As we would approach the refrain, I would encourage everyone to participate. For the "call," the song title is sung by the men in the deepest baritone voices they can muster. I lead the "response" with the help of the women. The final line of the chorus abruptly ends with a beautiful E minor chord and everyone singing in unison. Participants delight in how their voices resonate with the final chord on the guitar as they stop singing at precisely the same time. Invariably, they look around and smile. At that moment, they feel like professional singers. What's more, they feel a compelling sense of community.

At some point during our evening sing, two colleagues with preschoolers at the day care center located in our office building suggested I consider sharing my music with the children there. I'd never played any children's music live, even to my sons Charlie and Evan when they were young, but this sounded like fun. Before long, I was singing along with my guitar for thirty minutes every other week to a dozen four-year-olds.

The songs were different than the ones I shared with adults, but music's ability to energize the audience was much the same. When I launched into "The Ants Go Marching," these energetic preschoolers stood up and paraded around the room. One day, a child shouted, "Go faster!" I picked up the tempo while the children circled the big blue floor mat until they were completely out of breath, at which point I slowed the tempo to a crawl, my vocals sounding like a tape recorder with dying batteries. When

I speeded up again, the children's movement mirrored my tempo. This unique version of "kid aerobics" matched the experience I'd had with adults – the music united them, compelled them to move in unison, and created a powerful sense of community.

At the end of each session, the children would form a line to take turns strumming the guitar strings with my pick while I formed chords with my left hand. It made the musical experience more personal and real for them. On occasion, a mischievous child would intentionally insert the plectrum into the sound hole and drop it into the body of the guitar. Getting the pick out was a pain, but it was worth the effort because it engaged the children more directly with the instrument and me. I felt like a star to them. In return, they brightened my day.

The thirty precious minutes I spent with these little ones every other week became one of my most enriching experiences during my remaining months at work. I marveled at how they responded to the music and how much joy it gave them. Through these children, I found affirmation and authenticity that was often missing in adults, and I wondered how I was going to replace this after I retired.

In early 2008, I conducted a casual online search related to music and stumbled upon the topic of music therapy. I visited the websites of local universities to find out if they had a degreed program and checked out the course offerings and degree requirements. A few days later, I contacted Dr. Robert Krout, Chairman of the Music Therapy Department at Southern Methodist University in Dallas. When I shared my background,

Dr. Krout suggested I audit his Introduction to Music Therapy class, which I began attending that fall.

I enjoyed Dr. Krout's lectures and the way he pulled out his guitar to demonstrate a point he was making. I was learning more about the power of music to heal others when applied in a disciplined fashion. I was excited to discover empirical evidence to support its effectiveness in addressing a wide range of needs for diverse audiences. My intrinsic belief that music possessed therapeutic value was being expanded and ratified.

But there were challenges I was unwilling or unable to solve. The investment of time required to become a board certified music therapist (up to two and one-half years of course work at an approved university program) was more than I wanted to commit to.

I also questioned whether this discipline and my interests represented a good fit. Music therapists use elements like rhythm and tempo to achieve a wide range of non-musical goals like improving coordination, enhancing memory, managing pain, and supporting physical rehabilitation. Music therapy, I learned, was less about making music and more about using music as a form of treatment, observing and documenting its effects, and revising the approach. Work with a single client could be a lengthy and ongoing process, with therapists guiding their client's involvement via the use of music.

I was more interested in providing music for children and reaping the rewards that came from seeing an immediate response. My horizons were being broadened, but the field of music therapy didn't feel like the right direction for me to follow. Again, I pondered what path I should take.

One day, while roaming the halls before class, I noticed a small flyer announcing an upcoming workshop sponsored by a nonprofit group named Hugworks. "Cute name," I thought. The workshop title, "Make Your Music Matter More – Therapeutic Entertainment in Pediatric Healthcare Settings," sounded interesting. Of course I wanted to make my music matter more, and I already knew I loved playing for children.

The next Friday, when I arrived at the workshop, I took an inconspicuous seat toward the back of the room. Immediately, the two vintage Guild guitars resting on stands at the front of the room grabbed my attention. Seeing these cousins of my own Guild dreadnought on display created an immediate connection. Better still, their presence indicated live music would be shared during the presentation.

Once the workshop began, Dr. Krout introduced the "fearsome twosome" of Jim Newton and Paul G. Hill, who visited pediatric hospitals throughout the country. Dr. Krout explained how Hugworks and music therapy both provide children with positive experiences while they were in life-threatening situations out of their control. He described how he was partnering with Hugworks to teach therapeutic music entertainment techniques to SMU music therapy students.

After learning there were also volunteer opportunities available for adults like me, I was hooked. I began shadowing Jim and Paul around Dallas-area hospital waiting areas, playrooms, and individual patient rooms while they sang songs and interacted with children and their families and staff. Following each session, I asked for the rationale behind what I had observed in an attempt to make explicit what they'd been doing implicitly for years. In return, I was able to capitalize on knowledge they had gleaned from playing to more than 300,000 severely ill children and their caregivers over the past thirty years.

To complement what I was learning through Jim and Paul, I simultaneously entered the Music for Healing and Transition Program (MHTP) being offered for the first time in the Dallas area. The MHTP curriculum consisted of eighty hours of class instruction and outside readings designed to prepare musicians for providing live therapeutic music at the bedsides of the sick, the dying, and those who care for them. MHTP seemed like the perfect way to gain additional knowledge and insight into the realities of playing music for others in hospitals.

I followed these two complementary tracks toward building competence as a therapeutic musician for most of 2009. Their origins were different, but Hugworks and MHTP shared the same unwavering belief that music was intrinsically helpful in addressing emotional and physical needs in healthcare settings. An entirely new world was opening up to me and

I liked how it felt. I was learning how exceptional it is to bring music into the hospital. I saw how musical experiences can transform audiences as well as the musicians playing the songs. I was beginning to believe that providing live therapeutic music in hospitals was something I wanted to do.

By fall, I still had not played or sung to a single patient in a hospital, but on a Sunday afternoon in early October, that chance arrived. Theory became reality, and my life and outlook were forever changed.

# Chapter Two
## My Music Lesson

On a crisp October morning in 2009, I arrived at the large downtown medical complex for my clinical practicum. Today, I would step out of theory and into the all-too-real realm of the sick, applying my eighty hours of classwork into twenty minutes of what I hoped would be helpful and healing music for my first patient.

Seven of us had started MHTP together the previous February. We possessed varying degrees of musical competence but a common desire to use our gifts to help others. One class-mate was an accountant, three were schoolteachers, another was a stay-at-home mom, and one was a nurse. Only the nurse had spent much time in a clinical setting, and none of us understood what it would be like to provide music in a hospital.

Our inexperience made Judith Ritchie, area coordinator for the program, critical to our training. After completing the same program herself a few years earlier, she had begun practicing bedside music using a Plucked Psaltery capable of making a heavenly sound. Her instrument choice and long, graying hair offered clues that she was a child of the '60s. Her bright eyes shimmered behind her wire-rimmed glasses, and she talked of angels. I liked her immediately.

Since a different instructor taught each of the five program modules, Judith provided much-needed continuity. Whenever a topic drifted toward the esoteric or our questions bordered on naive, we could count on her to offer valuable insight.

The plan for this long-awaited day was straightforward. Five of us would play for adult patients in the main hospital in the morning while two others would wait until the afternoon to play at the small inpatient facility for children.

After receiving our patient assignments, we would each enter our designated room and ask for permission to offer music. Our instructor and one other student would stand at the edge of the room to observe. At the end of the day, we would share our experiences with the entire group, an approach that allowed us to learn from all the visits, not just the two we attended.

Given my interest in working with children, I asked to be assigned a child. I was delighted when my request was granted, but it meant I had to wait until the afternoon for my practicum playing experience, giving me lots of time to wonder and worry.

At long last, we walked to the children's facility a couple of blocks away that specialized in the treatment of young children with birth and developmental disorders. As we huddled in the second-floor hallway, Judith and our instructor sorted through an unanticipated complication. Both children on their list were boys, and the one assigned to my classmate was older than anticipated. In the belief that I, an adult male, might be a more appropriate fit for the teenager, they switched our assignments.

"Larry, you will play for a seventeen-year-old male who is in a coma. He is awake and alert and extremely agitated, but unresponsive," said the instructor.

What did this mean? I could understand how a patient might be "unresponsive," but the words "awake," "alert," and "agitated" did not fit the television image of peacefully sleeping comatose patients. Judith explained that people coming out of a coma seldom suddenly wake up and find themselves back to normal. The brain nerves start to fire, but in irregular patterns. Some patients, I learned, do not progress beyond this agitated state.

This was all the information I received, and it fanned the flames of my nervousness. I was used to singing for small children, not teenagers, and certainly not to agitated or comatose ones. How would I fill twenty minutes?

It may not sound like a long time, but if you've never played for a patient before, twenty minutes seems like an eternity.

Though I had no idea what to expect inside Jason's room, I did have a plan in mind. We had been taught to observe the situation and then select music based on that data. Given my lack of experience and limited self-confidence, I had decided before entering the room to play one or two soft ballads I'd known for years. This seemed like a safe and comfortable way to address the uncertainty of this first experience.

When I entered his room, Jason was sitting in a wheelchair, facing away from the door. The walls were decorated with a poster of his favorite college team along with get well cards and balloons, an indication that he'd been here for some time.

Jason's father stood hunched in front of his son, trying to feed him. His father encouraged him to take a drink, but Jason did not respond to his prompts. The man rattled the cup inches from his son's face, much like you might shake a toy in front of a pet's nose, hoping to capture his attention. Finally, Jason took a small sip through the straw.

I asked if it would be all right if I provided some music, and the father reluctantly agreed, slipping behind the curtain to the side of the room. He seemed impatient, and I sensed he was not excited at the presence of three total strangers in his son's room.

I turned toward Jason and noticed for the first time that he was buckled into his wheelchair. His agitation was manifested in his legs kicking wildly in the air. I told him I would play a song for him. He didn't respond, so I began with one of the ballads on my list, "As Tears Go By," written by Mick Jagger and Keith Richards of the Rolling Stones early in the 1960s. I chose this tune because I could extend the soothing melody for a long time, and I eased into it with gentle strumming, knowing I could adjust the musical direction depending on Jason's reaction.

The G chord that opens the song resonated throughout the small room. Immediately, it grabbed Jason's attention. He turned his head, eyes gazing slightly downward, and focused on the guitar and my playing hand.

After completing the verse and chorus a couple of times, I began to hum the tune. All the while, Jason's eyes remained fixed on the guitar. Somehow, the music was breaking through whatever barriers accompany a comatose state.

I was only a couple of minutes into the song when, to my astonishment, Jason raised his head, looked me directly in the eyes, and smiled like I was a long-lost friend he'd just rediscovered.

When I struck a misshapen chord a bit louder than expected, Jason chuckled as if he found my clumsy technique humorous. A few minutes later, he slowly folded his hands together in a manner that seemed to say "Thank you." Until now, his hands had been glued to his chair.

A true connection had happened – was happening – right now!

I glanced at my instructor, who was also moved, and impulsively decided to add vocals to the song in the hope that my voice might build upon Jason's positive response.

As Jason continued to concentrate on the guitar and my strumming, I noticed the father peering around the curtain, his face shining with tears. I wondered if he was experiencing joy because of Jason's response, was crying because of the lyrics, or both.

Still playing and singing, I silently began to question my song choice. I'd been so focused on my own nervousness that I'd overlooked the impact the lyrics might have on Jason's father. I had chosen a profoundly sad song that spoke of the emptiness of feeling disconnected from children and childhood. Perhaps these words expressed the father's deep longing for his son to be healthy again.

I played a second song, but I recall little about it. Having no idea how close I might be to reaching our twenty-minute target, I thought it wise to end the session. When I bowed to thank Jason for giving me the opportunity to play for him, I noticed that his body was relaxed and still. No more moving, shifting, or kicking. For the moment at least, he was at peace.

As I started toward the door, the father approached me and said, "He used to strum a bit, too."

I thanked him for telling me this and wished him well. I left Jason's room but made it no farther than the hallway before I broke down and cried. My sadness at seeing this beautiful young man in such a state had morphed into awe at the miracle of his response.

My instructor placed a comforting arm around me. Recalling the last-minute assignment change, she said, "You were meant to be here."

Back in our classroom that afternoon, we shared our experiences and then discussed the tasks we needed to accomplish in order to start our forty-hour internships. This was the next critical phase of the program, but I had a more immediate concern on my mind.

"What can I do for Jason now?" I asked.

Judith replied, "You might be able to arrange an internship at his hospital, but you must complete a final exam before that can begin."

This felt more like an obstacle than a requirement. I wanted to go back and visit Jason right away, whether I received official credit for doing so or not. Maybe the connection wouldn't happen again when I returned, but maybe, just maybe, it would be stronger and would be a real help to him. How could I not try?

I asked, "Why can't I go back and play for him sooner?"

"You're not ready," said Judith.

"But we made a connection today," I said.

"There's just no way to make it happen," she explained, adding, "I'm really glad you had this powerful experience so early, but it points out another self-care principle we teach in the program: if we get that attached to all our patients, we run the risk of burning out very quickly."

While I mulled this over, she said, "Yes, you did make a difference in Jason while you played for him, but you can't afford to think you can cure him or save him. That's up to God and Jason. What if you remain this wrapped up in him and he dies anyway? Where will your emotions be then?"

I felt like challenging the process, but I knew there was no way to argue with this voice of reason. I lacked the experience and competency an internship would provide.

Nonetheless, my overall perspective had changed. My twenty minutes of playing for Jason and his father had gone straight to my heart and confirmed within me the desire to follow this path toward therapeutic music. Before now, during our classroom sessions, I had wondered if I were truly capable of following this line of work. Hospitals and patients were a foreign world I'd been content to keep at a distance. I'd always been more of a sing-along leader adept at getting others to respond to familiar songs, but the connection the music had created between Jason and me was too remarkable to ignore.

Still, the more urgent matter remained: how could I get back to the hospital and play for Jason again? Maybe the connection wouldn't be repeated, but I couldn't let go of the idea that I should try.

As I studied my calendar, I noticed something that should have been obvious all along. Between my upcoming trip to Turkey to see my wife who was fulfilling a three-month teaching assignment, the approaching holidays, and the requirements I still had to complete, the earliest possible start of my internship would be February, more than three months away. Playing again for Jason was a remote possibility at best, but I couldn't help but wonder and wish for a way to get back to him sooner.

# Chapter Three
## A Painful Encore

Four weeks later, I was deep in the midst of packing for Turkey when the phone rang. It was Judith.

"Can you meet me at the hospital this afternoon?" she asked.

"I leave for my trip tomorrow," I replied, avoiding a premature commitment. "Why? What's up?"

"I can't tell you over the phone, but it's very important that you meet me here today if you can make it."

I considered the request, wondering why it was so shrouded in mystery. I couldn't help but think it had something to do with Jason, who was seldom far from my thoughts. "Okay. What time?"

"Can you meet me at the labyrinth outside the hospital at 1:00 p.m.?"

"Sure, Judith. I'll see you then."

"Great, Larry. Oh, and bring your guitar."

I didn't understand the secrecy, but I considered it Judith's way of hinting that she was inviting me to play for Jason. Was I going to get what I'd wanted all along? I had to contain my excitement over what might happen next.

When I met Judith at the labyrinth, she explained that the medications Jason had been taking had horrible side effects and that he had been placed on a ventilator. The tubes and machines that had been supporting his life had been removed, and his family and medical staff were searching for something that might help after this critical procedure. Recalling my initial visit, one of them had suggested I return.

I gathered my guitar and followed Judith into the main hospital, where we took the elevator to a floor in an older wing. The institutional green color of the halls was a stark contrast to the cheerful decor at the children's facility where I'd first met Jason a month before. It reminded me of the factory I'd worked at in the summers while in college and conveyed a sense of seriousness that set the tone for what would happen next.

After a short walk down the hall, Judith stopped in front of a door. "This is it. Don't be alarmed by what you see."

I nodded. Once again, I was unsure of what to expect. But unlike the first time I'd played for Jason, when I'd had time to weigh my musical options, this felt rushed. I had no idea what to play, and I chided myself. How could I have wanted this encore opportunity so badly without giving any thought to what I would do if it arrived?

When we entered the room, we found Jason lying in bed on his right side, facing the door. An adult woman, probably his mother, reclined behind him, supporting his body while stroking his shoulders and head.

Recalling his condition during my first visit, I took mental inventory. Yes, he was still comatose. No, he was no longer awake or agitated. His only movement came from his breathing. I watched as his chest heaved and fell in no particular rhythm or pattern.

I scanned the room and recognized the father standing to my right, shifting stiffly in position. The impatience I'd noticed during my first visit had given way to tension that told me Jason was not in a good place.

I faced Jason and asked him if it was okay for me to play some music for him. He did not respond. I glanced up at the monitor and noted his elevated and erratic pulse. I began strumming my guitar at a consistent sixty beats or so per minute, hoping this tempo would help regulate Jason's breathing and heartbeat. Replicating the musical approach from my earlier successful visit, I started playing a soothing ballad on my guitar.

There was no response. Instead, Jason continued to gasp and gulp for air, each breath a struggle. I added humming and then vocals and scanned the monitors, hoping to see some sign of response, but nothing changed.

After twenty minutes, maybe more, I began to wonder how much longer I should play. To continue seemed pointless. The teenage boy lying in front of me had been reduced to a series of numbers and patterns illuminated on a digital monitor. Still, when was it acceptable to give up?

As I pondered this question, a young man wearing a collar passed me, circled Jason's bed, and took a position facing me. I took this as an omen, a sign to bring the session to an end. At the end of the verse, I strummed one last chord, took a step closer to the bed, and leaned forward, whispering, "Goodbye, Jason. God be with you."

The chaplain followed Judith and me into the hall. We huddled for a moment, and then he put his arms around us both. As we stood in his embrace, he offered a brief prayer of hope and comfort for Jason and his family. Then, to my surprise, he petitioned God for my safe journey to see my wife. Somehow, this man I did not even know understood my personal plans and spoke words I needed to hear.

I welcomed both his blessing and his calming presence. Tears came to my eyes, not because I had witnessed the healing power of music but because a perfect stranger was taking the time to comfort me and tend to my needs.

I'd been given my chance to see Jason one more time, but I'd learned that Judith was correct – there are no guarantees the music will help. I'd been part of an extraordinary initial experience on practicum day, but it was now clear how rare this first experience might have been.

The next morning, I began my trip to Turkey. During my lengthy layover in New York before my flight to Istanbul, I noticed that the main terminal that had struck me as modern when I'd first visited JFK in 1973 now felt dated, dreary, and cramped. The gate waiting area was small and nearly full, so I sought refuge in a quieter place to finish reading the last two chapters of *Music as Medicine*, music therapist Deforia Lane's account of her life of music, healing, and faith. Sitting in a generic waiting area, I read this account of a comatose patient with terminal cancer:

> *Duane slipped into a coma, and the doctors said they could do nothing for him. Duane's devoted companion, a beautiful and gentle blond named Carol…played dulcimer music by his bedside every day. For weeks, Duane lay lifeless. And then, for no apparent reason, he awoke, living with much gusto for another year. Duane credited the music for punching a hole in his unconscious state. "I heard these beautiful notes," he would say afterward, "strains of music, and I had to find them. The sounds forced my mind to function as a mind should and not just sleep. They made me realize that out there was something worth looking for."*

I set the book down, my thoughts returning to the hospital room where Jason was fighting for his life. Thanks to Duane's description, I glimpsed what might have been happening on Jason's end while I played. Despite his lack of visible response yesterday, perhaps he had heard the sounds and felt a desire to search out their signal. Maybe the music had given him a pull, a reason not to give in to sleep. His lack of response during this second visit might not have been a failure at all. A positive outcome might only require patience, commitment, and time.

I promised myself I would find a way to return to Jason's room following my three weeks abroad to provide a musical tug that would penetrate his coma-muddled world and keep him searching and fighting for life. Yes, I would go back.

My flight was boarding soon, so I organized my backpack and made my way to the departure gate. Checking messages on my cell phone one last time, I noticed a missed call from Judith. Her message was brief.

"Jason passed away this afternoon, surrounded by his family. I thought you would want to know."

I didn't know what to think. My emotions felt pulled in so many directions that I decided it was safer to remain detached and move on, so I didn't respond to Judith's message. I simply boarded a plane I hoped would carry me to a place thousands of miles away from my sadness.

During the standard takeoff procedure a short while later, the flight attendant advised, "In case of an emergency, always put your own mask on first."

At that moment, it all clicked into place. I suddenly understood what might be called the "paradox of caring." That is, you are only able to tend to the needs of others by taking care of yourself first.

In the world of caregiving, the line that separates *caring* from *caring too much* is difficult to see. Sometimes it only becomes visible after you have crossed it.

I crossed this line with the very first patient I played music for. I was pulled back across to the other side by those who cautioned me not to cross that line in the first place, but I'm not blameless. I got exactly what I wanted: a chance to play for Jason again. I learned that therapeutic music is more than a classroom discussion topic. Patients are not classmates playing assigned roles. They are real people with real families, and their outcomes are real. Failure is real. Death is real.

I don't think I ever really thought I could cure Jason, but I was driven to try. Today, I believe that anyone who walked into his room on practicum day and played a few chords on a guitar would have witnessed the same awe-inspiring response. That belief gets me off the hook, erases my pride, and expunges some of my remaining regret.

But in the end, I *was* the person who, by God's providential hand, drew Jason's name that day. It was my great privilege to stand before him, play a few chords on my guitar, and witness his remarkable response. It was the most wonderful music lesson I could ever have hoped to receive, and in spite of my terrible sadness, I felt a new resolution to continue exploring the powerful connection a single song could make.

# Part Two

## From Sitting in to Going Solo

Through the Music for Healing and Transition Program, I received a comprehensive and personalized education in a very specialized field. I remained committed to providing music for children in the new and different context of the hospital, yet upon my return from Turkey, I balked at completing the internship requirement to become certified. I had the time available, but I lacked the psychic energy. The judgment that I had become too emotionally involved in the outcome of a single patient was correct.

Looking back, I believe much of my inertia stemmed from the realization that, after my music lesson with Jason, I would find it difficult to accept payment for providing such a beautiful gift to severely ill children. Becoming a certified music practitioner, earning compensation, and developing a new career had never been my goals. I was only looking for a meaningful place to play music for children.

Thus, Hugworks became the direction in which I channeled my energies. I embraced the mission to "bring the healing power of music to children everywhere," and Jim and Paul were open and welcoming. They offered me a window seat of sorts on a trip headed somewhere wonderfully new.

I began joining Jim and Paul at local hospitals as often as my schedule allowed. I learned through observation and discussion, and practiced and memorized their unique repertoire of songs written to convey messages severely ill children would benefit from hearing. Occasionally they let me "sit in" for them and offer a song to a patient. I benefited from this real-world experience followed by their immediate and encouraging feedback.

In early 2010, I set my sights on becoming Hugworks' first official therapeutic music entertainment volunteer. Little did I know how many rich experiences lay ahead. In the chapters that follow in Part Two, I convey some of these experiences as I watched, learned, and began to play for patients on my own, all the while marveling at the inherent power in a single song.

# Chapter Four
## Watching a Veteran

Today at the hospital...

...I again joined Jim for individual room visits. I wasn't ready to go out on my own yet, but I was getting close.

Jim and I stood together outside the eighth-floor room as he studied the small piece of paper listing the room numbers of patients the hospital's child life specialists thought might benefit from a visit. (Child life specialists are hospital employees with expertise in helping children and their families deal with the emotional and developmental challenges posed by childhood illnesses.)

Jim carefully tapped on the door, just loud enough to announce our presence without startling whoever might be on the other side, then opened it and peeked inside.

The child and her mother were both awake, so he entered and said, "Hello. I'm Jim. This is my friend Larry. We're here from Hugworks. The folks from child life thought you might like a song?"

The question surprised both the little girl, age ten or so, and her mother. Few choices are offered here, particularly ones like this. The girl sat up in bed and smiled, signaling her openness to the idea.

The mother was even more positive, something Jim told me he commonly sees because family caregivers are usually grateful for anything that breaks the tense monotony of the bedside vigil.

Having gained permission, Jim turned his attention to selecting the perfect song to fit the moment. We were surrounded by the latest medical technology. Instincts informed by thousands of room visits guided Jim's decision as he scanned the scene for clues.

The shades were open and the room was bright, suggesting something upbeat would be a good fit. Because mother and child were both present, a song that engaged them equally would be ideal. Jim cross-referenced these inputs against his mental list of original songs in the Hugworks' repertoire and arrived at his choice.

By now, he had positioned himself close enough to maintain eye contact with the girl but not so close that his large frame would seem imposing or threatening. He kept the mother in his line of sight, but her daughter enjoyed the front row seat. He looked at the girl and introduced his song choice with a smile, saying, "This song says the only thing you have to do to be the best you can be is… just be you."

The rich twelve-string resonance of Jim's guitar joined his molasses-smooth baritone as he began singing "I Can Be the Best I Can Be":

*I can't stand on a distant planet.*

*I can't stand on my sister Janet.*

*I can't stand on a rhino snout.*

*I can't stand Brussels sprouts.*

A smile crossed the faces of both mother and child. Such silly words! Little did they know that the humor of the verse was designed to set the stage for the message of encouragement conveyed in the song's chorus:

*But I can be the best I can be.*

*I can be the best I can be.*

*Take a look at me and you'll see*

*I can be the best I can be.*

*I can do the best I can do.*

*Yes, I can do the best I can do.*

*And I'm gonna bet you can, too.*

*You can do the best you can do.*

Mother and daughter smiled, trading quick glances with each other. Jim winked at the girl as he began the second verse:

*I can't drive a circus train.*

*I can't drive a big jet airplane.*

*I can't drive my dad to work.*

*But sometimes I drive...mom berserk!*

Both mother and child laughed at the honest human truth reflected in the lyrics. The music was yielding a positive moment they could share in a place where children and their parents don't always find much to smile about.

Jim repeated the chorus, followed by the bridge and the chorus for a third time. By the end of the song, the lyrics of encouragement "to be the best I can be" and "do the best I can do" had been repeated eighteen times, making it impossible to escape the song's central message, one that goes to the heart of the Hugworks mission "to bring the healing power of music to kids everywhere." The absurdity of each verse served as the appetizer; the chorus was the abundant main course.

Jim concluded the song and smiled at the little girl. The contemplative look on her face signaled that she was still processing the song's message and reflecting on what it meant to her.

"That was wonderful," said the mom. She clapped, and her daughter followed suit.

"Let's all give your best big round of applause," said Jim in an attempt to deflect the focus of attention back to the little girl. He added, "I hope you have a great today and an even better tomorrow. And I hope you always keep a song in your heart. It will make a big difference in how you feel…and how you heal."

Jim's wording was precise and intentional. He cannot promise a cure. Neither can the girl's doctors, the medical staff, or her mother. "Curing" is about fixing the body and making whatever is wrong go away. That makes a cure a matter of medicine and science. But Jim can provide words and music that help heal, or make whole, her spirit and soul.

As Jim and I exited their room, I couldn't help but feel we had left it a better place than when we'd arrived only five minutes before.

# Chapter Five
## Meeting Emerson's Future Classmates

Today at the hospital...

...I joined Jim and Paul for their bi-weekly visit to one of the larger children's hospitals in the metropolitan area. Shadowing them for a few months had made me more comfortable navigating this new world of hospital corridors and characters, but today's first stop reframed my perceptions.

When we walked into the Neonatal Intensive Care Unit (NICU), I was taken aback by the expansive openness of the space. Twenty, maybe twenty-five, patient stations were scattered throughout a room partitioned by medical equipment that served the dual role of monitoring the patients and defining a semi-private space for individual families. A single chair nestled within each space was the only place a parent could wait comfortably during visits and vigils.

The infants in the NICU require care far beyond what is provided on other medical floors. Most are dealing with heart, lung, and other abnormalities resulting from illness or premature birth. Not only is the ratio of healthcare professionals to patients higher here, but the number of specialized medical disciplines available for consultation extends far beyond the typical floor.

The latest technology was in place for these critically ill infants, and many would stay here for weeks, even months, placing enormous stress on their parents as they journeyed the long road toward health. Unfortunately, some of these babies would fail to make it home.

I was surprised we were allowed in this space until I saw Jim begin his work. "I'll handle this alone," he said quietly to Paul and me as he began strolling through the room like a troubadour. He played and sang at a soft and comforting level I had not thought possible given his resonant twelve-string guitar and deep baritone voice. His music was barely audible over the hum and whir of machines that provided a foundation of sound, but parents and nurses smiled and nodded in appreciation as he moved from one station to the next.

As I surveyed the scene, the NICU took on deeper meaning for me than it might have just a few weeks earlier. My first grandchild, a girl named Emerson, had been born in a different hospital two weeks before this visit. She'd arrived in this world normal and healthy. Within an hour of her birth, I was blessed with the chance to cradle her in my arms, and her parents took her home a couple of days later to begin the process of adapting to the new routines that accompany the birth of a baby.

By contrast, these NICU parents had to accept a distance enforced on them by treatment. I could not imagine how difficult it must have been to be unable to hold their tiny precious infants. While I stood in the corner of the room, the blessing I felt from Emerson's arrival was offset by the quiet intensity of this space.

As Jim completed his rounds, my emotions felt pulled in opposing directions. I gave thanks for my healthy granddaughter, but at the same time I found myself mirroring the uncertainty and fear these families were feeling.

I told myself that thanks to the miracles of modern medicine, these children had good odds of growing up healthy. Someday, they might even become friends with Emerson. That was a big assumption, but I was willing to set all expectations aside and wish them the best as they fought to overcome the medical challenges that lay ahead.

Today at the hospital, I witnessed how the comforting music Jim shared inside the NICU brought a warm and personal touch of humanity that prevailed over the cold and sterile machines designed to support the lives of these newborns. I felt honored to be there.

# Chapter Six
## Getting in the Way

Today at the hospital...

...There was excitement in the air when Jim and I arrived at our first stop on a central Texas hospital tour. Since the Hugworks team was only able to reach this children's hospital once or twice a year, the event was always well publicized. Sure enough, posters adorned the hallways and a local television station crew was on hand to cover our service of song to the children.

Inside the hospital, the child life specialist introduced us to the TV crew comprised of a female reporter and a lone cameraman. After exchanging greetings, Jim described our plan. We would start with a group sing-along in the playroom followed by visits to individual patient rooms. Once we had completed our rounds, Jim agreed to a personal interview so he could share the purpose and mission of Hugworks.

Following our twenty-minute session with five children and their family members, we headed for the rooms of those children unable to make it to the playroom. I followed Jim to our first stop, where he introduced us and offered a song.

During the first verse, I sensed the camera peering over my shoulder, searching for a scenic angle to capture the boy's reaction from my vantage point. As we began the second verse, the cameraman made his move. Hoping to get footage from the reverse perspective, he cut through the small pathway between us and the child's bed where he continued to film until we finished. Our song complete, we smiled and said goodbye to our delighted audience.

As we returned to the hallway, I considered our visit to be a great success. The perfect song had been nicely delivered to a happy child, and the faces of both the reporter and cameraman mirrored my positive assessment. They had captured the moment on film and now had a "feel-good story" to deliver on the local evening news about the program offered in their community.

But that triumphant moment was short lived. Once we were beyond earshot of the patient's door, Jim squared around to face the cameraman and said, "I know you have an important job to do. I'm grateful you're here to cover this story, but I'm here for these children. So in the future, I would ask you to avoid getting between the children and me because it interferes with my ability to bring music directly to them. In that way, the children can get what they need from the music, and you still get your story."

The cameraman nodded his understanding.

Today, I witnessed a core principle underlying the work we do in the hospitals: nothing should get in the way of the service we provide to the children. While it is gratifying to receive recognition in the form of press coverage, it should never be allowed to interfere with the needs of the children.

There was only one star of our little show today, and it was neither Jim, nor me, nor the worthy goal of creating a positive story. The star was the little boy we sang for. Therapeutic music entertainment is not about the performer or the performance, but about the children.

Today, I was reminded that I still have much to learn.

# Chapter Seven
## The Gift of Control

Today at the hospital...

...I had my first opportunity to visit individual patient rooms on my own.

In theory, I was well prepared. I'd followed Jim and Paul on numerous occasions over the course of many months, observing and asking questions about everything from how they introduced themselves to how they bid farewell. In spite of this, by the time I reached the first door the child life specialists had suggested, I was anxious about the prospect of providing live music to a total stranger. Jim and Paul made it look easy, but seeing is nothing like doing.

I stood in the hallway, reviewing the patient census over and over, perhaps as a way to delay my maiden solo attempt. I considered the child's age, gender, and length of stay. In this case, my first visit was to the room of a young boy who had been here almost a week, long enough to understand the ways of the hospital.

By shadowing Jim and Paul, I had come to understand that matching the right song to each child is critical to an effective therapeutic music session. Since the ability to make a quick and appropriate song choice requires experience, something I did not yet possess, I began to mentally review the criteria I might use to guide my selection. While the data captured on the patient census is useful, a quick scan of the room for environmental factors offers the best insight into what type of music might be appropriate. A darkened room suggests something quiet and calm like a lullaby. Open shades indicate a more positive and optimistic atmosphere and a livelier, more upbeat tune.

Stuffed animals, sports team banners, and balloons are also worth noting for their evidence of interests outside the hospital, but the best source of insight into what might be appropriate is the hospitalized child. Facial expression, skin pallor, posture, and level of consciousness provide a wealth of information. Alertness level and eye contact, or the lack thereof, represents windows into the child's emotional state. Of course, a sleeping child is never to be interrupted.

Soon, I realized this thought process was merely delaying my purpose for being here. I was spending time and energy considering what song to play before I'd even gained permission to provide one. Gathering my courage, I approached the door, knocked lightly, and opened it enough to peek inside.

"Hello, I'm Larry," I said. "The folks from child life told me you might like a song."

An adult woman who I assumed to be the child's mother smiled and said to the boy, "Look, a guitar. Maybe he'll play something for you." But the young lad shook his head and returned his attention to the television.

"That's okay," I replied. "I'll bet he doesn't get to say 'no' to much here, so if he would rather not have a song, that's fine with me." I excused myself and continued to the next room on my list.

My stops at the next couple of rooms mimicked the first. I asked if the child within would like a song only to be politely turned down. At the end of my rounds, I counted at least five children who had refused my offer of music even though the adults present had encouraged them to accept.

Jim had impressed upon me that placing the children in charge, empowering them with the right to refuse a song even if their parents think it's a good idea, is a core tenet of therapeutic music. In other words, the child's vote matters most.

But these experiences also demonstrated how easy it could be to take rejection personally, to consider it a sign of failure. I reminded myself that there's no room for a line of thinking that places my needs above the needs of those I come to serve.

Today at the hospital, I was reminded that I am here for the children. In that context, rejection is not a bad thing but rather a positive outcome. Severely ill hospitalized children are thrust into unfamiliar circumstances beyond their control where they are offered few if any choices. In this environment, honoring their wishes by giving them the gift of control may be as good for them as providing a song.

I look forward to more rejections in the future.

# Chapter Eight
## Foot-Tapping Music

Today at the hospital...

...I had the opportunity to play for a boy about twelve years old. He was positioned comfortably in his bed when I entered his room. He was alert and seated upright, with blankets and sheets wrapped firmly around him from the waist down.

When I asked if he would like a song, he nodded politely, but that was it. His face was expressionless, and he didn't make eye contact.

Experience has taught me that children in the preteen phase of life aren't always enthusiastic about the idea of a stranger singing to them, and that was precisely the vibe I was receiving now.

I'm not certain what it is about this development phase that leads to such reticence. Perhaps it's the growing sense of independence that comes with adolescence, an increasingly critical eye toward adults, or a preference for their own choice in music that results in the kind of ambivalent response I was getting. Regardless, when he agreed to a song, I was happy to provide one and hoped for the best.

I scanned the room for clues as to what song might be most appropriate for his age and mood. The curtains were pulled open, allowing the brightness and warmth of the day to bathe the area with light. Given his alert state, I decided something upbeat might work, and I began to play one of the first Hugworks songs, simply yet aptly titled, "Inside."

"Inside" has a bouncy feel that fits the song's positive lyrics. Inspired by the adage "you can't judge a book by its cover," each verse uses simple metaphors like a pie or birthday gift to communicate that appearances are less important than what lies beneath the surface.

As I played through the first verse, the lad stared ahead, making no eye contact. His face remained emotionless as I continued into the song's second stanza. I looked for a sign of enjoyment or rejection, but neither appeared. His blank and emotionless face stared toward the wall to my right.

I approached the end of the second verse, the halfway point in the song and a good place to take stock on whether to play the third verse or proceed right to the closing bridge and chorus. I was leaning toward the latter course of action, fearing the metaphors might be too juvenile for his age. But then, out of the corner of my eye, I noticed a slight movement beneath the blanket. It was the unmistakable evidence of the boy's right foot tapping in perfect time with the music – a sign of active engagement that belied his stoic face. It was all the encouragement I needed to play the third verse before continuing through to the end.

Jim Newton once told me, "There is always a response to the music. You just need to know what to look for."

He was right. Sometimes the evidence is clear, arriving in the form of a smile or tear. On other occasions, it remains mostly hidden inside the child. But more often than not, music seems to have a way of moving us even when we're trying our hardest to resist its power. It's a compelling reason to keep coming back, even when the only response is a foot moving stealthily in time with the music beneath a hospital sheet.

# Chapter Nine
## Upon Reflection

Today at the hospital…

…I stopped by the room of a boy who looked to be around eleven or twelve years old. After introducing myself and confirming that he'd like to hear a song, I decided to play the Hugworks tune, "Wouldn't It." I'd learned that children are often self-conscious about how their sickness and hospitalization makes them different from their friends, and I liked this song because it encourages them to look at being different in a more profound way.

Like many of the songs composed by Jim and Paul, there's a touch of playful whimsy in the arrangement. The lyrics use metaphors that can easily be understood by kids, allowing them to readily access the deeper messages. Each verse poses variations on a simple theme: wouldn't it be a shame if all the colors, all the seasons of the year, even all ice cream flavors were the same? The conclusion of each verse laments how sad such a world would be and shows how, through our differences, life becomes interesting.

I started to play. In spite of my best efforts to engage him, the boy remained decidedly passive, so much so that I couldn't figure out how, if at all, he was relating to the music. Though he seemed alert and was sitting up in bed, his facial expression never changed. Unlike the former pre-adolescent boy I'd played for, whose foot had been tapping under the sheet, I could detect no response whatsoever.

Halfway through the song, I began wondering if this boy's lack of response signaled dislike, either for the song or perhaps his situation. Since I knew the payoff came in the final verse and he wasn't visibly rejecting what I was doing, I decided to continue:

*You're the friend that I like best*

*Except, of course, for all the rest*

*And when all is said and done*

*We could be friends with everyone*

*Wouldn't it be a shame*

*If we were all the same…*

What he didn't know was that the final chorus ends with two additional short words that hang there, leaving listeners with something to consider and reflect upon:

*Wouldn't it be a shame*

*If we were all the same…Wouldn't it?*

I finished the song with this tag question, and to my surprise, the boy looked directly at me. In a straightforward, matter-of-fact way, he said, "Yes, it would."

I felt a sense of gratitude. He'd not only gotten the message but he was taking it seriously.

I appreciate the intentional messages behind the songs I play. I always try to select melodies that best deliver what I sense is needed by the audience, but this is an inexact art. Sometimes I leave a room without a clear impression that the desired meaning has gotten through. In these instances, I take comfort in knowing that live music from an unexpected visitor provided a momentary distraction. Meanwhile, I continue to hope that as the child reflects on the song, he or she "hears" the intended message.

But today offered more than that. This young boy was with me every note, every word, every beat of the way. What I'd interpreted as disinterest was actually a more immediate and deeper level of contemplation than I usually witnessed. This reflective boy taught me not to judge but instead to trust that the songs will do the heavy lifting, delivering their helpful and healing messages.

# Chapter Ten

## What Do You Do When the Music Can't Do Enough?

Today at the hospital...

...I made my first visit alone to the Intensive Care Unit (ICU). I had assumed the most seriously ill patients might be off-limits to non-essential visitors and to complementary treatments like music, but the child life specialists had included three patients in the ICU on their recommended list, so I headed to that floor.

Outside the unit, the large double doors limiting access opened to let a nurse exit. Because I wasn't certain my volunteer badge offered me access, I slipped in.

The cluster of nurses stationed on the inner side of the hallway circling the floor offered the first clues as to why the care here is termed "intensive." While other floors in the hospital are designed to ensure the privacy of patients and their families inside their rooms, the ICU seemed guided by the opposite goal.

The rooms were gated with big, sliding-glass doors left open to allow a clear line of sight and easy access. Here, everyone seemed to be on guarded watch, making the environment anything but relaxing.

The child in the first room appeared to be around twelve months old. I have always been proud of my ability to accurately estimate the age of young children, but in the hospital, sickness and treatment can conspire to delay physical and mental development. I double-checked the patient census and noted that the boy was eighteen months old, half a year older than I'd guessed.

He was alone in the room, so I approached his bed quietly, wondering where his family might be. I found him lying awake with numerous tubes attached to his small body. I told him my name and asked if I could play a song. Though he said nothing, he stared back with eyes that seemed slightly more welcoming than fearful. Taking that as a yes, I played a soft lullaby while humming rather than singing the words. There was little response. When the song was over, I bade him farewell and returned to the hall, leaving him as I'd found him, silent and alone.

If this first visit was the calm, in the next room I encountered the storm. From outside the door, I could hear the young child weeping. A nurse stood over her on one side of the bed, her mother on the opposite side. When they looked up, I asked, "Do you think a song might help?"

The mother gazed back at me without expression while the nurse replied, "They speak no English. But it's worth a try."

I decided to continue the ballad I had been playing in the previous room, but at this the little girl cried out in her native language. The mother stroked her shoulders while whispering words of comfort, but neither the music nor the mother's touch calmed the child. I looked down and noticed the line of sutures running like a railroad track along the length of the little girl's torso. Her pain must have been unbearable.

After a few moments, the mother looked at me and nodded. I took this as a sign to keep playing, but within less than a minute, it was clear the music was doing no good and was perhaps contributing to the child's response. By now, she was nearly screaming. I continued playing while I slowly backed into the hallway. The child's wailing faded into the distance as I moved down the corridor.

I took a deep breath, practicing a technique to help prepare me for the next visit. I visualized the scene from the last room, packed it into a mental compartment, and shipped it out of conscious thought, at least for the moment. Much like a baseball pitcher who gives up a home run or a quarterback who tosses an interception, my goal was to blot out the event in order to make the next throw with confidence. My purpose was not to ignore or forget what had taken place but to set it aside so as not to bring any residual anxiety into the next room.

When I arrived at the room of my third ICU patient, I found a nurse checking the array of monitors attached to a four-year-old girl who was lying on her side, facing away from the door. I asked the nurse, "Do you think she would like a song?"

"Yes," she responded. "But why don't you move over to the other side of the bed so she can see you?"

When I reached the far side of the room, I was taken aback by the bruises around the little girl's face and upper body. Her skin had a bluish hue. While it does me no good to possess information regarding what causes injuries like these, I couldn't help but consider the possibilities. It saddened me to see her lying so peaceful and still.

I started to play "If I Could," Paul G. Hill's beautiful composition that expresses almost in the form of a plea the singer's desire to provide friendship, a song, and a smile to someone in need of emotional support. As I entered the bridge of the song between the second and third verses, I choked on the words:

> And if I could
>
> I would stop the pain from ever getting through
>
> I would keep this world from ever hurting you
>
> If I could

Unable to sing, I played my guitar through the final verse and immediately headed for the door. In the hallway, I leaned back against the wall as tears rolled down my cheeks. It wasn't the sight of this last child that caused me to come undone, but the cumulative effect of being with three of the sickest small children I had ever seen, one after another after another.

I had learned from playing to Jason in the hospital that music has its limits. Today served to remind me of that reality. Even though I wished otherwise, there was nothing I could do to take away the pain of these three innocent sufferers. The music could only do so much.

Today at the hospital, it couldn't do enough. By extension, neither could I. There had to be something else. Something more. But what?

# Part Three
## Exploring New Boundaries

After a couple of years of singing for sick children in the hospital almost once a week, I felt more comfortable in the role of hospital musician, but it was often an uneasy comfort.

Some days, I honored my scheduled commitment to play more out of a sense of responsibility than mission. I sometimes noticed what felt very much like relief when I found the child I was to play for was asleep or doctors were present, circumstances that meant "do not disturb" and that I was "off the hook."

Overall, I was coming to realize that my relationship with this work was more of an uneasy truce than a solid alliance. On my worst days, my lack of confidence led me to focus more on what I was doing and how I was feeling than on the audience I was there to serve. Even on days when I felt more confident, I often felt unfulfilled when the music produced an indifferent response. My initial experience playing to Jason had been so powerful that I unfairly expected every musical encounter to be as positive.

Still, in spite of my ambivalent feelings about the contribution I was making, I continued to show up. I deeply admired the children, and I marveled at how well most of them handled their situations. I developed a deep sense of caring for these children and their families that I could not shake. I began to feel that a single song wasn't enough, that they needed more, and that I did, too.

In early 2012, a casual comment opened my eyes to a new possibility. I was a member of an informal advisory group established to support a visiting pastor at our church. Over lunch one day, I mentioned my volunteer work in the hospital as a Hugworks musician. Martha, the visiting pastor, asked, "Have you ever thought about CPE?"

"What is that?" I asked. I had no idea what the initials stood for.

Martha described how CPE, or clinical pastoral education, is a form of theological education that takes place in clinical settings, typically hospitals. She explained that most seminaries require their students to complete one unit of CPE before graduation, although a number of laypersons also participate. She added that the instruction and clinical experiences focus on the needs of those who receive care as well as the study of one's self in the role of a practicing caregiver.

"You should consider it, Larry," she concluded. "After all, you're already going to the hospital."

Over the next few weeks, I thought about Martha's comment. I couldn't shake the feeling that there might be more I could do to serve the children and their families, but at the same time, I didn't know what direction that service might take. I also found myself struggling with the notion of how anyone can truly discern direction in life.

The following week, I dropped by the adult Sunday school class I occasionally attended to find an associate pastor discussing what "vocation" and "calling" mean for Christians. The words she read from Barbara Brown Taylor's book *The Preaching Life* hit me head on: "There is simply no getting around it. If the church is where we learn who we are and whose we are, the world is where we are called to put that knowledge to use."

Immediately following this class, I walked to the morning worship, where the senior pastor opened his sermon with comments about his CPE experience as a seminary student and the impact it had on his view of himself and his ministry.

Could it be mere coincidence that multiple sources were suggesting the same direction at the very moment I was most open to receiving it?

I decided the answer was no. After conducting additional research, I decided to request an application for the eight-month extended CPE program at the same children's hospital where I served as a musician.

Filling out this application required a great deal of reflection and sharing personal history. The question that challenged me most was rather straightforward: "Provide an account of a helping incident in which you were the person who provided the help. Describe how you became involved and what you did. Give a brief, evaluative commentary on what you did and how you believe you were able to help."

It bothered me how difficult it was to think of a meaningful "helping incident." To be sure, I had counseled co-workers and direct reports during my career. I had helped a stranger change a tire once. My service as a musician in the hospital certainly counted for something. Nonetheless, I couldn't think of anything big and meaningful to share, so I wrote about the most recent example of helping someone that came to mind.

One of our pastors had asked my wife to help a woman in our church who had separated from her husband. Sandy and I had taken care of their young children on a couple of occasions when work conflicts had prevented the parents from getting home at their usual times.

While Sandy facilitated finding friends to provide meals for Cindy and the children, I began driving four-year-old Caleb to and from day care a few days a week, something that formerly had been the responsibility of the husband. The task was easy to perform, given my fairly flexible schedule, and being Caleb's chauffeur became my way of helping Cindy.

Initially, Caleb was upset when separating from his mother, but over time, this became easier for everyone. Eventually, the child welcomed me warmly when I arrived to pick him up in the late afternoons.

After fulfilling this duty for a few weeks, both our senior pastor and the head of the day care thanked me for what I was doing for Caleb. Their comments surprised me and illustrated one of the mysteries associated with serving others: it isn't always clear who is being helped the most. In this case, was it Cindy? Was it Caleb? Was it me? Was it somehow all of us?

A couple of months after writing about this experience, still mulling over my application to the CPE program, I was able to travel to Chicago for a two-day visit with my parents who live south of the city. My wife had told them in her regular email updates how I was driving Caleb to day care each week. When this topic came up in our conversation, my father opened his Bible, pulled out a sheet of paper, and handed me a short poem that he said made him think of what I was doing for Caleb. The first two verses read as follows:

> *We shall do so much in the years to come,*
>
> *But what have we done today?*
>
> *We shall give our gold in a princely sum,*
>
> *But what did we give today?*
>
> *We shall lift the heart, and dry the tear,*
>
> *We shall plant a hope in the place of fear,*
>
> *We shall speak the words of love and cheer,*
>
> *But what have we done today?*

At the time, I didn't know where my father had found these verses, though I've since learned they are from the poem "We Shall Do So Much in the Years to Come" written by late nineteenth and early twentieth-century poet Nixon Waterman. I only knew these words spoke to me about the need to translate good intentions into something specific. "What *have* I done today?" I wondered.

That fall, CPE became the next phase of my journey. It was something I believed would be a natural extension of what I was already doing through my music, and hopefully a way for me to more effectively practice the art of helpful caregiving to others.

As the following essays in this section reveal, the term "practice" came to take on a certain irony. Despite the fact that I had no experience in the role, the ID badge I was given on the first day of the program read "chaplain," with the word "intern" conspicuously absent. I wondered where this new road might take me and whether I truly understood what I'd signed up for in entering the clinical pastoral education program.

# Chapter Eleven
## Dual Identity

Today at the hospital…

…I shadowed Randall, an experienced chaplain who graciously allowed me to tag along with him on visits to patients' rooms. While I had made hundreds of visits in this hospital as a musician, I did not know what to expect in my first experience seeing this world through the eyes of a chaplain.

When we entered our initial room, two parents greeted us. The uneasy manner in which they moved suggested a high level of anxiety. Meanwhile, their young son, lying in his bed watching a movie on TV, appeared calm. There were no balloons or cards in the room, no pillows or blankets on the daybed, so I surmised the child might be a recent admission to the hospital.

A minute or so into our visit, I realized I had provided a song for this same family about five hours earlier as a Hugworks volunteer. I wondered why it had taken me so long to make the connection, but it appeared the family didn't remember me either. Was it my introduction as "chaplain" versus "musician" that prevented us from recognizing one another? Or did my wardrobe change from a brightly colored shirt to a dress shirt and tie do the trick?

I watched closely as Randall eased the parents into meaningful dialogue, asking, "So what brings you to this place?"

The parents told him about their child's recent diagnosis, and Randall probed further, assessing their mindset and needs along the way.

"How are you handling the news? Do you have support from friends and your church family?"

His questions were direct and to the point but posed with sensitivity.

After their discussion, Randall turned to the child, who was relaxing in bed. He engaged him in small talk, asking about the movie and his favorite characters. The little boy answered with comfortable enthusiasm.

Turning back to the parents, Randall offered an insightful observation and suggestion for them to consider. "You know, your son seems to be handling all of this very well so far. A thought for you – maybe you can take your cues from how he is feeling. If he is doing fine, then maybe you can be less anxious yourselves. There may be a time when he is not feeling so well and will need you to be strong for him. You can support each other in that way as you go through all of this together."

The parents nodded, signaling their understanding.

Later, I reflected on the contrast between this visit and the one I had made to the same room earlier in the day. I had noticed that the adults were more anxious than the child, but my visit had intentionally been brief, allowing time for only an introduction and a single song with no room to explore this observation further or assist in any lasting way. Noting how Randall had handled himself, I could envision how, in the role of chaplain, it might be possible for me to go beyond the music and have a meaningful discussion with a child or family members.

I did not mention my earlier visit to Randall or the parents. I wasn't sure it would matter to them, but it mattered to me. I had entered the clinical pastoral education program feeling it was important not to involve my music in the chaplaincy experience. I expected there would be a day, sometime much later, when I could consider the similarities and differences between the two identities and allow them to inform one another, but for now, I simply wanted to learn how to be a more effective listener and to gain a deeper understanding of how to assess and respond to the needs of those who found themselves in the hospital.

# Chapter Twelve
## A Good Waiter

Today at the hospital...

...Was my first night on call. For the next fifteen hours, I would be the only chaplain at this major trauma center. I feared I wasn't up to the task.

My peers and I in the clinical pastoral education program called ourselves "externs," short for "extended interns." Though we had received basic training on hospital policies and procedures and I had benefited from shadowing two experienced chaplains during room visits, I did not feel ready to be in "the big house" alone. Our training thus far had not covered specific tools and techniques to help me navigate this foreign clinical world.

Whenever I suggested that I lacked sufficient formal training or credentials to wear a badge that read "chaplain," the response was consistently the same: "We would not have accepted you into the CPE program if we did not believe you were qualified to do the work."

Meanwhile, my supervisor had a knack for coming up with helpful metaphors to illustrate key pastoral care principles. He likened our concern about our inexperience to the story of the cowardly lion in *The Wizard of Oz*, explaining, "His search was to find the lion already inside of him. Each of you is on a journey to find the chaplain you have already become based on your life experiences."

As I started my initial shift as an on-call chaplain, this metaphor seemed to suit me well. Tonight was my premier, starring in the role of the "cowardly chaplain." Strapping the pager to my belt, I feared it might begin to shriek loudly at any moment. Simply anticipating its shrill pitch and the urgent, cryptic message on the tiny screen was enough to raise my anxiety level.

Thirty-five minutes into my assignment, the pager announced a code blue in the radiation department – someone needed immediate resuscitation. When I arrived five minutes later, the hallway inside the department was already crowded with at least twenty doctors and nurses, an impressive and immediate response. In the middle of the crowd, I could see four or five individuals grabbing equipment from the crash cart. Although I stood about twenty feet away, an unmistakable sense of urgency surrounded the scene.

As I looked toward the action, a gentleman wearing a dress shirt and tie came to my side. I don't know if it was the unsure look on my unfamiliar face or the fact that I was also wearing a tie that prompted him to say, "You stand here," as he pointed to the wall on my left. I thanked him for the advice.

After a few tense minutes, word began to filter back that the three-year-old boy whose airway had collapsed during an x-ray was breathing on his own. Groups of doctors and nurses began to exit the scene, leaving the core team to continue caring for the child. A woman who had been standing next to me said, "Let's go see the parents. They're in the waiting room." I read the words "social worker" on her badge.

We found the parents seated together in the waiting area of the radiation department. After brief introductions, we began our trek to the ICU where their child would be taken. The father glanced at my badge and asked, "How long have you been a pastor?"

I could not think of a good way to answer this simple question. If I told him I wasn't a minister, I feared losing the credibility that came with the title on my identification badge. But if I gave him an answer containing an actual time frame without further explanation, I might be implying that I was indeed a pastor. I felt like I was in the grips of a double bind with no way out, so I simply responded, "I am fairly new here at the hospital." This sufficiently vague yet truthful response seemed to satisfy his curiosity.

For the next hour, I followed these parents around the hospital as they signed forms admitting their son and updated family members by phone. Standing a few feet away but always in view, I worried that they might wonder about my constant but silent presence. Despite being hesitant to initiate my first pastoral care conversation, I also did not want to intrude.

When the father and mother finally took seats next to each other in the waiting room, I reintroduced myself, knelt before them, and asked, "Are you two okay?"

They both nodded yes.

"Do you need me to do anything for you right now?" I asked.

They indicated they did not.

The look in their eyes revealed the power of the moment. These simple questions provided their first opportunity in over an hour to take inventory of their own emotions. The questions served as a pause button, providing them license to consider their own needs. Still, I kept wondering if I had waited too long to introduce myself.

When I shared this experience with my supervisor a couple of days later, he suggested that my restraint might have been exactly what these parents needed.

"You know, Larry, others might not have been able to wait that long. They might not have been able to keep their own need to speak in check. You waited until the moment was right."

Naturally, he offered another metaphor to help illuminate the event and my role. "A good chaplain," he said, "is like a good waiter in a restaurant. He knows how to provide attentive service without being overly bothersome. I think you were a good waiter that night."

In reframing what I considered to be my own inadequacies into a positive event from which I could build, my supervisor gave me the confidence I needed to continue as a chaplain, cowardly or not.

# Chapter Thirteen
## The Devil in the Details

Today at the hospital....

...I had just begun my on-call assignment when I received a page to visit a room on the seventh floor.

When I arrived, the door was open, so I knocked and walked in.

The patient, a teenage girl, was sitting on the bed, facing away from the door and staring at her cell phone. A woman I assumed was her mother was sitting in a far corner, engaged in a conversation on her cell phone. An older man, likely the grandfather, stood and walked toward me. I sensed immediately that he would be the focus of my visit.

"Hello," I said. "I am Chaplain Larry from the pastoral care department. Is this a good time for a visit?"

This was the first time I had introduced myself as "chaplain." That may seem like a minor matter, but earlier in the week, the head of the department had overheard me mentioning to my peers that I was hesitant to introduce myself using that title.

"So what *do* you call yourself?" he'd asked in a voice laden with sarcasm. His tone left me surprised that he hadn't fired me on the spot, even though that would have been difficult to do, since I wasn't getting paid.

"Why are you here?" the man asked, his question suggesting that he had not requested a chaplain visit.

I had learned that on some occasions, hospital staff will request that a chaplain speak to someone they find difficult or are unsure of how to handle. I had a feeling this might be one of those situations.

"I'm hoping I can be of some help," I answered. "So, what brought all of you here to the hospital?"

"We are here by the grace of God," the man answered. "My granddaughter went to visit her friends in the afternoon a few days ago. When she didn't come home when we expected her to, I went out looking for her and found her at a friend's house passed out on the floor. She had been drinking all afternoon and her blood alcohol was way over the limit. We have been here now for three days."

"It's only been two days," said the girl, revealing that she was paying as much attention to our conversation as she was to her cell phone.

"No, we have been here three days," corrected the mother.

"Yes, three," echoed the grandfather.

"Did I come by helicopter? That would have been cool," said the girl.

I couldn't help but think she was in search of something interesting to post on her social media page, and I tried to process that thought without judgment.

"No, we came by ambulance. You were so out of it you wouldn't have remembered the ride," said the mother.

"Is there anything I can do for you at this time?" I asked the grandfather in an attempt to return the discussion to something that might have a beneficial outcome.

"Maybe pray for us," he said.

When I started my time as chaplain, I feared the possibility of having to pray out loud for someone until my supervisor provided a useful suggestion: "Ask what they want you to pray for," he said. "They will tell you. Your job is to listen carefully and raise their concerns and fears to God on their behalf. You don't have to say anything fancy, just what is important to them."

"Sure, I can do that," I said to the grandfather. "What would you like me to pray for?"

"For safety," he replied.

I recognized this answer as encompassing a lot of history and other emotions. In my CPE training, I had also learned not to assume that any given word means the same thing to everyone. During our small group discussions, one colleague had described how he'd prayed for "a miracle" because that is what the family had requested. Our supervisor had asked, "Did you know what 'a miracle' looked like for that family? Was it a cure? Could it have been an end to suffering? A big part of your role is to try to find out."

It was reflective learning like this that made the CPE program so rich and at times so personally painful.

"Why do you say 'safety'?" I asked, seeking clarification so I'd know exactly what I was to pray for. "Are you afraid of something?"

To my surprise, the grandfather responded in the affirmative. He explained, "In my work, I was required to study Satanism and devil worship. I never talked to my granddaughter about it. Eventually I got rid of all the materials I had brought into our house. I've had a hard time the past three years or so," he continued. "I still have my faith, but I think he is with us all the time."

While I tried to process this, he explained, "Weird things started to happen in our house. The other day..."

"Wait," I interrupted. "Can we go back a bit? When you say 'he is with us,' are you talking about God or the devil?" I assumed he meant the former, but I needed to be certain.

"The devil," he said matter-of-factly.

"And you think he is behind the 'hard time' you are going through?" I asked.

"Yes," said the grandfather.

I was glad I had asked for clarity. Though it felt impolite to stop him mid-sentence, backing up in our conversation was a critical step toward my understanding and ability to offer a genuinely helpful prayer.

Before I said my prayer, I asked the girl to put down her cell phone. "We can talk directly to God without it," I told her. Then I proceeded to give thanks for the love of those close to her —her mother, her grandfather, and her hundreds of Facebook friends – and prayed for all of them to feel God's strong presence surrounding their family.

I had always considered myself to be a good listener during my professional career, but listening in the hospital requires a keener and more acute attention to specifics. The stakes here are higher because the current conversation might be the only opportunity to hear what is troubling a person. Often, like today, the devil is in the details.

# Chapter Fourteen
## Lighten Up

Today at the hospital...

...I received unexpected feedback with unusual timing from a surprising source.

I was on call when a trauma case brought an extended family to the emergency department to support a set of parents whose child was in peril. I positioned myself outside the family consultation room next to five or six members of the group.

As a chaplain, I was not always privy to detailed medical information, but I had enough experience in the role to read the signs. It was taking much longer for the doctor to appear and give us an update than we'd been told it would. This was worrisome, but we waited together patiently, anticipating a diagnosis that would either confirm or relieve our deepest fears.

In situations like this, time slows down so completely that it evaporates from consciousness. Matters of life and death bring to the surface existential questions that defy the predictable structure of time measurement.

I stood in my finest stoic fashion, focused on the weightiness of the moment and the likely tenor of the upcoming conversation. As I contemplated what I might say or do should the worst possible news arrive, an aunt interrupted my thoughts with a question that jarred me back into the moment.

"Why are you so serious?" she asked with a wry smile.

I did not know what to say. This was a serious situation, and I felt I was reflecting that reality, but was my sober manner detaching me from the family members standing around me? I wondered if I truly understood what this family needed at the moment. The best response I could muster was a modest smile.

Meanwhile, my mind raced back to a hospital visit I'd made eight years earlier to my assistant, who was suffering through the final stages of terminal cancer. I had put off the visit for a few days, failing to realize how sick Chris really was. When I arrived, we talked for about twenty minutes while she floated in and out of consciousness.

I was uncomfortable, and my impatience eventually got the better of me. When I sensed it might be a good time to make my exit, I whispered, "I will be going now."

I'll never forget how Chris grabbed my arm, looked me in the eye, and said, "It's okay."

Assuming she was referring to the fact that I hadn't paid her a visit sooner, I said, "I'm sorry."

But Chris always had a unique way of spotting and naming the truth of any situation. She tightened her grip so I couldn't escape, looked directly at me, and said, more emphatically, "Lighten up!"

"What?" I asked.

"Lighten up!"

Chris was gone within a couple of days, faster than any of us expected, but her direct message to me has hung around ever since. I know now she was making a much larger point, reminding me to stay positive in the face of troubling events, loving me enough to try to make me a better person even as she left this world.

I am still troubled by the fact that my visit to her came so late. I like to think she would be proud to see how far I have come, that the hospital is now a place where I feel increasingly relaxed visiting and serving others. But still I wonder why I'm able to comfort strangers in a manner I could not do for a dear friend. Did I allow my closeness to her get in the way of being present for her?

Today, I gained insight into why many hospitals now welcome clowns, dogs, and even musicians. Some families may need distraction instead of silence, good cheer in the face of fear.

Perhaps in the darkest of moments, a little levity has its place, and a positive and supportive presence is more helpful than a somber and stoic one.

Today at the hospital, two people separated by time and circumstances, one who'd just met me and another who knew me well, one who stood in my presence and another who stood in my memory, both reminded me to stop taking everything so seriously and to "lighten up."

Upon reflection, I can't help but conclude that maybe I haven't come so far after all.

# Chapter Fifteen
## Recorded in Red

Today at the hospital...

...I sat staring blindly at the image of the Excel spreadsheet projected on the wall of our cramped meeting room.

Chaplains take turns reading entries from their weekend on-call assignments in order to update everyone on what has happened in the hospital since the office closed the previous Friday. I'd come to dread this aspect of my chaplain responsibilities, but this particular Monday morning review was the most anxiety-producing thirty minutes I'd ever experienced.

"Larry," said the chaplain leading the discussion, "it appears you had a busy night this weekend. Could you read for us?"

I didn't know where to begin. There were multiple entries with my name next to them, all made between Saturday evening and the following Sunday morning. Most were recorded in red, the color used to indicate decedent care activity.

I decided to start with my last entry, made around 10:00 a.m. Sunday morning, two hours after my shift was scheduled to end. Using the cryptic language we had been taught, I read:

Sunday. 3:10 hours. E.D. Daniel R. 15 months old. Arrived by CareFlite. Patient died from injuries related to motor vehicle accident. Medical examiner declined case. Chaplain provided pastoral presence during family viewings in morgue.

Then I stopped, lost in thought.

Before this weekend, my only visit to the morgue had been on our tour of the hospital during our first week of CPE training, almost four months earlier. Though the on-call assignments of many of my colleagues had taken them to the morgue, I wasn't certain I could even find it. Listening to them describe their decedent care experiences, I felt inspired by how they'd handled themselves and the resilience they'd demonstrated afterward.

"I'm still in!" declared a fellow extern after sharing details of an extremely difficult situation. I wondered if I'd be able to hold up so well. When I took the on-call pager at 5:00 p.m. Saturday afternoon at the start of my shift, little did I know I was about to find out.

The evening began quietly enough, but the office phone rang around 9:30 that night. A mother was calling to provide funeral home information for her son who had died at the hospital two days earlier.

I expressed my sympathy and explained that I would need to call her back. The hospital's decedent care policy states that if this information is provided over the phone, the presence of a witness is required to verify. I apologized for the bureaucratic delay and told her I would call back in the next thirty minutes.

I wasn't sure who I could find to witness her call at this hour since the hospital halls become rather desolate this time of day. I ran upstairs to the first floor front desk. When I mentioned that I needed someone to help me on a case involving a child who had passed away, the woman at the desk asked, "You mean this family?" and pointed to four adults behind me.

"No," I corrected her, a bit flustered. "The parents I am working with called on the phone."

The receptionist located a security guard to join me at the pastoral care office. Together, we returned the mother's call and recorded the information on the "Release of Body Authorization" form bearing the child's name.

As I hung up the phone, I heard a knock on the office door. When I opened it, I faced the group of four adults I had seen upstairs minutes before.

"Our daughter's body is in the morgue," said the father. His demeanor was straightforward, not emotional, and for that I was grateful. "Her grandparents are here, and we would like to view her body before it is taken to the funeral home tomorrow."

This explained the earlier confusion at the first-floor reception desk.

I had never before seen a body in the morgue, but common sense suggested something needed to be done to prepare it for viewing. Still, nothing in my decedent care training had described a scenario like this.

"Why don't you sit in the family waiting room next to our office while I make the necessary arrangements," I said, not certain what those might be.

While the family sat in the small room, I phoned the on-call supervisor, who instructed me to contact the hospital's head nurse on duty and ask for her help preparing the body for viewing.

The hospital morgue is comprised of two divergent worlds. The area in the back is brightly lit, its stainless steel tables and cabinets emitting a sterile feeling devoid of emotional content. The cooler where bodies are held until they are released takes up a corner of this room.

This world is accessible to only a few hospital staff, and for good reason. No parent is allowed to enter this space, and I doubt any would want to. Their space is the family viewing room, a carpeted room with comfortable chairs and dim lighting.

While I fulfilled my chaplain duty of signing the in/out record posted outside the cooler door, a team of nurses began the task of transforming the cold corpse of a little girl into a warm presentation for loved ones to view.

A short while later, as I stood with the parents and grandparents of this child, I marveled at the careful work of the nurses. By wrapping and surrounding the small body in blankets, they gave a sense of dignity to the scene, leaving a positive lasting image of a beloved child and hopefully a degree of closure for the family.

After a few minutes, I escorted the family back to the lobby while the nurses started to reverse the process, preparing the body for its return to the morgue body bag. I then returned to the morgue to sign the record posted outside the cooler door, something that is required every time a body is placed in the cooler or taken out.

It was a bit after 11:00 when I returned to the pastoral care office, took off my shirt and tie, and lay down in an attempt to sleep. My two experiences this evening had been sobering, but I felt a sense of gratitude for having been eased into a chaplain's decedent care responsibilities in a calm yet meaningful manner. In both cases, the families had already reached some level of acceptance over their loss, minimizing the rawness of their grief and pain.

For the next couple of hours, I tossed and turned in a futile attempt to sleep. I tried a few mental tricks I hoped would quiet my active mind, but nothing worked. I couldn't stop thinking about the two families and their deceased children.

At 1:30 a.m., the on-call pager cried out; a nurse was requesting my assistance. There is no delicate way to describe her request or my assignment.

The surgeons had finished harvesting tissues and organs for transplant from a deceased child, and the body was ready to be returned to the morgue. A little red wagon, the kind children play with every day, was needed for the task, and so was someone to pull it.

These wagons are a common sight in the hospital during the day, serving as tiny limos that carry small passengers with their belongings as they arrive or leave the hospital. Even though the chances of anyone seeing our trip at 2:00 a.m. were slim, one of these wagons covered with blankets would provide a stealth vehicle for transporting a small body to the morgue.

I found a wagon near the main lobby reception area and headed upstairs where the nurse would meet me. As I stepped out of the elevator, two medical personnel wearing surgical scrubs and toting coolers stepped in. I chose not to consider the contents of those coolers.

The nurse joined me as we delivered the red wagon to the morgue. She handled the body while I took care of the sign-in sheet. I then returned to the office and again tried in vain to sleep.

Within an hour, at 3:10 a.m. to be precise, my pager shrieked again. The message on its tiny screen read:

Trauma alert. 6 yo male. mva. arr 10 min. CareFlite.

Once again, I threw on my shirt and tie and headed for the ED. Within five minutes, I arrived through the back door and signed the trauma support team sign-in sheet posted next to one of the critical care rooms. I then took my position in the short hallway with the other non-medical staff. We waited for the paramedics to arrive through the double doors at the end of the hallway that open to the ambulance bay.

As we stood in anxious silence, the hall space was bombarded with a choir of pagers singing the shrill A note in unison. In synchronized motion, we looked at the small screens on our pagers:

Trauma stat. 15 mo male. mva. arr 10 min. CareFlite.

Was this a correction from the previous page? Had the level of urgency changed? The person to my left looked as puzzled as the one on my right. What was going on? At that moment, our pagers sang out again:

Trauma alert. 9 yo female. mva. arr 15 min. ambulance.

The double doors flew open as the paramedics guided a gurney into the first critical care unit on their left. The child on the gurney looked like he might be about six. He had a few cuts and abrasions around his face but appeared alert as the doctors and nurses tended to him.

A moment later, the doors to the ambulance bay burst open again. This time, the gurney carried a small child. In that moment, we all discerned the answer to our confusion over the multiple similar pages we had received – three pages, three siblings, one motor vehicle accident.

A second team of doctors and nurses began their work in the adjacent critical care room. From my vantage point in the hall, I could not see what was going on, but I sensed the urgency in their actions and voices. A couple of minutes later, a nurse inside shut the sliding door to the room, completely blocking our view.

"That's a bad sign," commented the social worker standing next to me.

Soon the third child arrived, thankfully looking much like the first. Word spread that the parents were in the hospital next door and that family members would be arriving soon. I kept an eye out for them, and about a half hour later, an aunt and grandmother arrived. I showed them to the family room where we waited for someone to inform us of the status of the children. Finally, a nurse came in to provide an update.

"The older children are doing well," she said. "But the youngest is not. There is nothing more the doctors can do now. Would one of you like to go see him?"

The aunt consented and followed the nurse into the critical care room. Allowing at least one family member to view the scene provides a mental image that helps dispel any notion that the doctors could have done more to save the patient. I sat with the grandmother, who buried her head in her arms and sobbed. Moments later, the aunt returned to tell us Daniel was gone.

For the next hour, I worked through the list of responsibilities that the chaplain handles when a death occurs. As additional family members arrived, I provided directions on how to navigate between here and the adjoining hospital where the parents were being treated. I had no idea if the parents were in any condition to hear that their child had died, and I was unsure whose responsibility it might be to tell them. As I wondered what to do, I received a page from the chaplain there, providing the phone number where I could reach him. When I called, he told me the parents already knew about their son's death.

I expected the family members here would want to view the child's body, but since this death met multiple criteria to qualify as a case for the medical examiner's office (the child was under the age of six and had died of unnatural causes within twenty-four hours of arriving at the hospital), it was important to know if the office had accepted the case. According to the decedent care checklist in our training materials, this decision would dictate the limitations that would be placed on the family while viewing the child.

More specifically, if the medical examiner's office accepted the case, I would need to make sure that no one disrupted the equipment that remained attached to his tiny body. I hated the thought that enforcing these restrictions might be up to me.

When a nurse told me the little boy's body was ready for transport to the morgue, I asked that it be prepared for a viewing by the aunt and grandmother, a process I had first learned about only six hours earlier.

When the body was brought into the viewing room, I stood behind the relatives as they stared at the small child lying before them. The aunt placed her arm around her mother, the grandmother, in an attempt to hold her upright and together. It was excruciatingly painful to witness their grief.

After about twenty minutes, they told me they were ready to leave. I escorted them back to the emergency department family room while the nurses carefully placed the infant's body in a bag to take it to the cooler. A short while later, for the fourth time in fewer than eight hours, I wrote my initials on the sheet posted outside the morgue cooler door. It was 6:30 a.m.

I thanked the nurses for their help and took a deep breath. Before I returned to the family room where I had left the aunt and grandmother, I intended to check on the other two children. I knew they were in good hands with the nurses and child life specialist on duty, but I was sorry I hadn't had a chance to talk to them. As I turned the corner into the hallway, I saw the social worker heading in my direction.

"Get ready," she said. "The mother was just discharged from the hospital next door. She is coming here now, and she wants to hold her son."

I closed my eyes briefly, trying to brace myself for the grief I was about to witness.

Within a few minutes, the mother arrived, sitting in a wheelchair pushed by another relative. I introduced myself and asked for her patience as I went to the head nurse to tell her we needed to repeat the process we had just completed and prepare the child for another viewing.

The head nurse was more accepting of the request than I had expected and asked me to wait a couple of minutes. She wanted to assign the duty to another team of nurses now arriving to begin their 7:00 a.m. shift.

I then called the medical examiner's office to ask what limitations I was obligated to place on the mother's desire to hold her child. I felt torn between the restrictions I'd read about and my desire to honor a mother's need to grieve.

To my great relief, the woman on the other end of the phone said, "Give her some lee-way. We are not going to take the case. It was clearly an accident."

I escorted the mother and five other family members to the morgue waiting room. Finally, the child was brought in, his body surrounded by blankets. As the mother's wheelchair was pushed to the side of the table, she rose gingerly and cried out her son's name.

"Daniel! Daniel! Why didn't I let you leave with your aunt? Why did I keep you with us? Why did this happen? Why? Why?"

She bent down and kissed his face. She cradled his tiny body in her arms. The medical equipment the trauma surgeons had attached to his body as they fought to save him lay covered by blankets below his feet. It prevented her from picking him up completely, but she was holding him nonetheless. It seemed to be enough for her.

The mother's agony was palpable; the scene continued for what seemed like an eternity. As I stood there, I became acutely aware of how I ached from head to toe. Unbidden thoughts came that I tried to push away, thoughts like, "I wouldn't be mourning like this, for this long. When will this end?"

My CPE training had helped me learn to consider this judgmental inner voice an expression of my own biases and beliefs, a potential barrier to being fully present to others. Recognizing this voice allowed me to consciously set it aside so I could focus on the grief-stricken mother. With an effort, I pushed away my awareness of my own exhaustion.

When I felt my pager vibrate again, I looked at the message, surprised to find it was already past 8:30 a.m. Laura, the chaplain scheduled to follow me on call, had arrived at the pastoral care office minutes ago.

"Where are you? I am in the office," read the pager message.

I hadn't been back to the office since I'd left for the emergency department more than five hours earlier, and I hadn't thought to leave a message about my whereabouts. I slipped into the back room of the morgue and called Laura telling her I would return when I was done with the current case, though I had no idea how long that might be.

As I rejoined the grieving mother, I wondered again when she would be ready to put the child down. Then I realized the honest answer was, "Never."

A nurse whispered to me, "The body is getting warm. We need to return him to the cooler soon."

I didn't know what to do. The mother's grief was so profound that there was no way I could interrupt it. Despite how tired I felt, I had neither the desire nor the know-how to bring the scene to an end.

I looked at the social worker who had joined us. Perhaps sensing the need to guide the family toward closure, she sat down by the mother and said, "Let us give you a couple more minutes alone with him before we all go."

It was the most sensitive way to handle the situation I could have imagined.

Sometime after 9:00 a.m., I arrived back at the pastoral care office. The pullout bed was still open, the sheets crumpled on top. It seemed like centuries since I'd lain beneath them.

Laura was waiting in the corner. I handed her the pager, sat down beside her, and wept. Somehow, I'd held my emotions in check in the face of a stampede of grief unlike any I had ever witnessed. Now, exhausted physically and emotionally, I poured them out with my tears until I felt empty inside.

Laura encouraged me to talk. She prayed for me, and it helped me deal with the trauma I'd observed and personally felt. Each time a feeling of self-pity rose inside, I knocked it down with the recognition that compared to what these families were going through, my pain was insignificant. The image of the mother bending over, holding her child only inches off the table to kiss him one last time, would not go away.

Laura took the pager from me and headed to the emergency department to follow through on the items on the decedent care checklist I had not started. All that remained for me to do was make multiple entries in the pastoral care contact log describing the parade of death that had passed my way that night and how I had attended to family members' needs:

> Sunday. 3:10 hours. E.D. Daniel R. 15 months old. Arrived by CareFlite. Patient died from injuries related to motor vehicle accident. Medical Examiner declined case. Chaplain provided pastoral presence during family viewings in morgue.

Suddenly, I jolted back to the present with the realization that I was holding up our Monday morning review. I looked around at my fellow chaplains and supervisors. All eyes were on me, expectantly waiting for me to share my thoughts.

"Did you find the decedent care checklist helpful?" asked one of them.

"Yes, I did," was the only thing I could find to say.

I remembered how the frigid December air had warmed the bitter chill inside me as I walked toward my car upon leaving the hospital. I recalled feeling like a different person than the man who'd begun that on-call shift, but I'd known what I needed to do to regain my sense of wholeness.

I needed to go home, see my family, and somehow come to terms with a night that, in my heart, would forever be recorded in red.

# Chapter Sixteen
## A Great-Grandmother

Today at the hospital...

...The pager was thankfully silent. No requests for room consults were waiting on the fax machine in the pastoral care office, so I checked the census to see if a young patient I had met three days earlier was still in the hospital. He was, so I decided to pay an unannounced visit to his room in the ICU.

I had been on call the prior Thursday when Marcus arrived at the emergency department via ambulance after a tragic incident in which he'd been oxygen deprived for an unknown period of time. The small boy was accompanied by his great-grandmother, who made the hour-long ride with him. There was a feeling of peacefulness in her presence despite the situation. I escorted her to a family waiting room where she could call to update family members in private.

Within an hour, ten to twelve members of the extended family had begun to arrive. I'd found it difficult to take an exact count, because they arrived in shifts and there was no single room where all could assemble. I scurried back and forth between the family waiting room and the critical care unit where the medical team was working on Marcus, trying my best to be a calming presence.

At one point, I noticed a young woman comforting another. I assumed she was part of the family, but when I stopped to talk, I learned she'd come to the emergency department that night to be with a different family but had felt moved to comfort a stranger in a time of great emotional pain. This young lady might not have been wearing a badge bearing a title, but her act of compassion struck me as exemplifying what it truly means to be a chaplain.

After all of Marcus' family was present, I noticed how everyone directed their concern toward the great-grandmother. Did she need anything? Had she brought her meds with her? Was she staying hydrated?

When my peers and I studied "family systems theory," we were told that families can be like puzzles and that it can take time to identify their interpersonal dynamics and conflicts. In this family, all emotional energy seemed to pass through the great-grandmother, and it was energy of the most positive and supportive kind.

For the next four hours, I helped the family navigate from the chaos of the emergency department to the solitude of the small consultation room outside the ICU. Here, time slowed to a crawl as we sat together, fully present in the raw emotion of the moment, waiting for a doctor to arrive, hoping he'd tell us our worst fears about Marcus' condition were misguided.

Finally, the doctor appeared. "He is very sick," he said, stretching out the word "very" for emphasis. "We have him sedated. You can go see him now."

Since regulations limited the number of ICU room visitors to two, I shuttled family members to Marcus' room one at a time. I left the hospital the next morning, but the great-grand-mother remained at his side, a constant presence.

Returning to the room three days later, I found her still seated by Marcus' bed.

"I was wondering where you were," she said. Seeing a pillow and wrinkled sheets on the daybed to the side, I suspected she hadn't left the hospital since her arrival.

As we talked, it became clear that she was walking a tight-rope of hope, that fine line between faith in God's healing hand and acceptance of the reality of Marcus's medical condition. She told me she feared the worst, and I asked if I could pray with her. When she nodded, I thanked God for her strength and love for the life of her great-grandson. She seemed comforted by my words.

As I stood to leave, I asked about the rest of her family.

"They are all downstairs in the first-floor waiting area," she replied.

When I stopped to visit, I was surprised by the scene. Fifteen relatives, maybe more, were watching TV, grazing on snacks, playing board games, and laughing.

I heard the familiar voice inside my head immediately pronounce judgment on the festivities. *My family would not act like this under these circumstances*, it said.

Once again, I was relieved when my training kicked in and helped me cast this inner voice away. This was not about my family and me. I was here to offer support, not judgment.

As I continued watching these individuals, the scene slowly began to feel right. When two middle-aged aunts saw me, they waved for me to join them. After a few moments together, I began to feel like part of their family. They fully welcomed me, and I felt their acceptance and love. After a time, I excused myself from their warmth before the moment became any less perfect.

A few days later, I shared this story with my supervisor. I suggested that it represented a key element of the chaplain's role: knowing when your work is done and sensing the appropriate time to leave.

The supervisor saw something more significant in my connection with this family. He was aware of the degree to which I'd come to feel these hospital halls were a wilderness my CPE commitment required me to wander through. By inviting me to be in community with them, this family had tended to the loneliness I felt in the role of chaplain. In words reflecting the story of the Good Samaritan, he said, "Larry, suddenly perhaps you were the one lying injured on the side of the road, and the family was the stranger who stopped to help."

Marcus left this world the following Tuesday. I never had a chance to tell him how blessed he was to have been born to a family full of such dedication, love, and hospitality, but I did have the opportunity to tend to the needs of his great-grandmother while the rest of his family tended to mine.

I think I may have gotten the better end of the deal.

# Chapter Seventeen
## An Empty Vessel

Today at the hospital....

...I was preparing to settle down in the pastoral care office to try to get some sleep, though sleep is tough to come by here. As late as it was, the anxiety of anticipating a pager alert, periodic foot traffic outside the door, and the uncomfortable pullout futon couch conspired to forestall any attempt at rest.

On this particular evening, I wasn't the only one anticipating a sleepless night. A nurse from the seventh floor called, telling me a mother wanted to meet a chaplain in, of all places, the chapel.

I told the nurse I would wait for the woman outside the chapel door, and I positioned myself in the hallway to wait.

There were no visitors in this lower-level corridor at this time at night, only a pair of janitors pushing whirring machines that cleaned and polished the floor. They ignored me as I stood in silence, anticipating the upcoming conversation. The woman's request to meet in the chapel was unusual, and I wondered why she had chosen this hour. She must be religious, I decided.

Within a few minutes, a small Hispanic woman with tears filling her eyes appeared. We exchanged greetings while I opened the door and gestured for her to enter ahead of me. Inside, she paused to scan the room before selecting a front row pew. I sat directly beside her, and she immediately slid over to the next pew, a move that altered the physical distance between us by only a couple of feet but created an immense emotional gulf.

I asked her what I could do to help her, and she shared her story. Her sister had passed away recently and she was still mourning that loss. Now, her young son lay upstairs in a bed and was connected to a respirator.

"I am looking for an answer to just one question," she said, turning to look directly at me. "What must I do so God will make all of this go away?"

At a loss to reply, I asked the woman about her son, her sister, her family. I attempted to explore her emotions. I inquired about her faith experience and her supporting relationships. I learned that she had not been raised in the church and had no system of religious belief.

"That is why I am here," she said. Then she repeated, "Tell me, what must I do to make this all go away?"

I thought back to the theology paper I had presented to my fellow externs the week before. I had titled it "Walking

Beside Others: A Theology of the Journey" because it explored the parallels between my chaplain experiences to date and my month-long walk on the Camino de Santiago (a pilgrimage route across northern Spain) the previous summer.

I had written, "The times I felt I came closest to fulfilling the promise inherent in the chaplain title were when I walked beside strangers in their time of greatest need. I comforted them. I offered my hospitality. I sat beside them in silence, in part because I am a man of few words but mainly because I knew of no words that could provide the answer to the questions reflected in their tears."

I told the woman she was not alone, that in the hospital, everyone from chaplains to those of little faith seeks an answer to the question, "Where is God in all of this?"

But her tears continued to flow, and she kept coming back to the same question: "You are a pastor, so you must have the answer. What must I do?"

*I am not a pastor, only a naïve, well-intended layperson trying to help others,* I thought to myself. But I knew that description was no longer entirely accurate or helpful.

I suggested that she would need to find the answer herself, that this would require a journey, and that I would help her along the way if she liked, but my words failed to address her desperate need.

I tried to ignore a sinking feeling deep inside. My theology was being exposed for what one of my more fundamentalist fellow externs had declared it to be when he said, "I found it hard to relate to. I mean, you wrote about journeys but failed to express any firm beliefs. It seems you have no North Star to guide you."

Those comments had devastated me and fanned the flames of the insecurity already burning inside me, but this situation was worse than any criticism a colleague could offer. I was seated next to a woman who was asking me for exactly what my peer said I lacked. Accordingly, I provided her no answers, only additional questions.

I tried to get her to tell me more about her family, but every avenue I explored became a blind alley that seemed to make matters worse. When I asked about the small necklace she wore, she told me it was a gift from her sister and that it reminded her of how they'd fought shortly before her sister's death.

"I am sorry," was the only response I could find.

We talked another twenty minutes or so, and when the time felt right, I prayed that God would help her in her journey to find meaning in all that was happening to her and her family. I then escorted her to her son's room. We stood by his bed, watching him lie in the peaceful stillness of the darkened room, and more tears were visible in her weary eyes as I left. I don't think either of us got much sleep that night.

Memories of this encounter visited me often over the next few days. It was apparent that this mother was looking for a manual, a recipe, a set of directions she could follow that would cure her son and heal her wounded soul, but I had no such guide to give her. I brought a "theology of the journey" into our conversation that offered no concrete answers to the existential questions she posed, and I concluded she was an empty faith vessel I was unable to fill.

I considered this "empty vessel" metaphor to be apt because she had asked me to "fill" her with my version of the truth. I've since learned that Plato originated the "empty vessel" phrase by writing, "An empty vessel makes the loudest sound, so they that have the least wit are the greatest babblers."

I now wonder if today at the hospital I, too, was an "empty vessel" because I talked but had neither the wit nor wisdom to provide the answers she sought.

# Chapter Eighteen
## Finding a Blessing

Today at the hospital...

...I began my final on-call assignment as chaplain. It was a gorgeous sunny Sunday afternoon, and my shift started at 3:00 p.m. In my heart of hearts, I would rather have been almost anywhere else in the world, but I had signed up for this time slot, and it was my responsibility to be here.

I tried to find positive energy in the fact that, at ten o'clock tonight, my eight-month odyssey through the CPE program would end, my clinical responsibilities would conclude, and I would hand off the pager for the last time. I was walking an emotional line between the anticipation of finishing and the fear of what I might be required to do in the next seven hours.

I prayed for a quiet day, but almost as soon as the pager hit my hand, it began to vibrate. A nurse on the fifth floor was requesting a chaplain. When I arrived, she pointed to a couple occupying the small alcove in the corner.

"Their son is being moved to the ICU this afternoon," she told me. "They know no English, only Spanish. They are very upset."

The father was seated while his wife paced the adjacent hall talking on her cell phone in her native language. I knew enough Spanish to make a cordial greeting and small talk with the father, but I recognized that any conversation in the hospital demands a level of accuracy and sensitivity that stretched far beyond my limitations. I asked the nurse to request one of the hospital's translators to help, but this was a Sunday, and there was no translator on the premises. Instead, we would be connected via phone with a translator who would help us with our discussion.

A nurse set a landline telephone on a small table between our chairs. With the help of the translator, I introduced myself to the father and asked about his son. In response, he told me his teenage son's condition was getting worse, not better. I followed up with more questions and tried to explore how the father was feeling, but his answers became increasingly terse and his face more sullen, almost to the point of anger.

His growing frustration with the situation and the clumsiness of our translated conversation reminded me of the discomfort I'd felt in my late night discussion with the young Hispanic mother three nights before. Again, it seemed, I was unable to find a way to connect with a person I had been called to comfort.

During our extern readings, I had been introduced to the concept of "the middle realm," an emotional space where two human beings are able to join together in a common spirit. This is more than a neutral zone, I learned. It is a place that is neither yours nor mine but rather is ours, a place where we both can be fully present in relationship with one another, where effortless conversation and emotional healing can begin.

I had hoped to experience this "middle realm" during my clinical experience. I was confident I would know it when I saw it, and this clearly wasn't it. On the contrary, the telephone sitting between the father and me marked the vast emotional divide between us.

As I considered what I might do to try to improve the dynamics surrounding our conversation, I recalled advice I had received near the start of my chaplaincy experience: "Families are your best source for finding out what they need."

In an act that might be described as informed desperation to salvage something from our visit, I decided there was only one question left for me to ask through the translator. More a plea than a question, I said, "Please, can you ask him if there is anything, anything at all, I can do right now that would be helpful to him and his family?"

The question captured the father's attention, and his response was immediate and clear. He said, "I would like a priest to offer a blessing on my son."

I knew immediately what to do. Having passed by the hospital chapel hundreds of times, I recalled the sign indicating the Spanish language mass held there every Sunday afternoon. I could not recall the exact time of the service, but I excused myself, saying I'd be back soon, and headed to the chapel to find someone who could help.

When I opened the door, I felt like my own silent prayer had been answered. In a building designed to isolate disease and suffering into individual rooms, a priest was conducting mass in Spanish to the largest crowd I had ever seen occupy the chapel.

I stood near the last row as worshippers came forward to accept the elements of the Holy Eucharist. I worshipped with them as best I could, but I was anxious for the service to end. My thoughts drifted toward what I might say to convince this priest to follow me to the fifth floor.

When the service ended, most worshippers headed toward the exit. Others moved forward to help the priest return the chalice, paten, candles, and linens to a small storage closet to the side of the chapel.

I waited for the crowd to thin before I approached the priest. When I was within five feet of him, the short woman in front of me turned to make her exit and smiled at me before I recognized her. It was the same troubled woman I'd sat with in this same chapel three nights before.

"How are you?" I asked.

"Better. Much better," she said. "Thank you."

I wanted to find out what had changed since our talk, but I was intent on my new mission to assist a troubled father who I feared might be doubting my return.

I stepped up to the padre, a short bespectacled man in his sixties.

"Excuse me, Father," I said. "I am the chaplain on call. There is a teenage boy who is a patient on the fifth floor. The family only speaks Spanish, and the parents have asked if it would be possible for you to bless their son."

"I know that child and his family," he replied with enthusiasm. "Let us go to them now."

Moments later, I stood at the end of the bed as the priest and parents exchanged greetings and took their places around the child. The priest consoled the parents in language they understood, and his words of comfort were clearly what they needed. As he performed the Catholic sacrament of Anointing the Sick, I watched as the face of the boy's father was transformed from an expression of deep despair into one of abundant hope.

I left the room thankful I had been a small part of a helpful outcome. I personally had not done anything particularly meaningful, but I believe some greater power led me to ask that father the right question and directed me to the place where I could find help. As a result, perhaps by chance but more likely through providence, I was able to honor a father's request for a blessing and in the process receive the blessing I needed to bring closure to my clinical chaplain experience.

The father's blessing came in the form of a priest able to offer a meaningful sacrament, while mine arrived in the form of a broad smile of gratitude from a woman I'd feared I'd failed three nights before.

The remainder of the evening was quiet. When I handed the pager to my replacement a few minutes before 10:00, I felt a deep sense of relief that my clinical experience had come to an end. There would be no more on-call assignments for me. It was time to start mentally unpacking the baggage I'd accumulated during the past eight months.

It was time to move on. The question was, to where?

# Part Four
## My Road Back to Music

Once my chaplain responsibilities were complete, I returned to the hospital only twice in the next eight months. The first time was to attend a brief graduation ceremony and return office keys; the next was for an end-of-unit evaluation discussion with my supervisor. On both occasions, I exited the building as quickly as possible.

For me, the clinical pastoral education experience had followed an emotional arc from anticipation to self-doubt and finally to isolation. My interviews with pastors and friends who had completed CPE training had told me quite clearly what I might encounter, but experiencing it was vastly different from hearing about it.

Taking on this new challenge and discovering I was not cut out for it was difficult for me, someone accustomed to succeeding at whatever he tried, and the experience raised basic questions. Why had I signed up for this? What did I learn through the process? What would I take with me going forward?

Being the chaplain on call had forced me to consider matters of life and death I had been content to avoid. The model of learning used in CPE encouraged me to act and then reflect on my interactions with others to gain a deeper perspective on their needs and how I had helped. This approach facilitated rapid growth and personal learning. It was also painfully efficient at helping me understand what I am made of and where my boundaries lie.

Nonetheless, I recognized that my unit of CPE training had provided some of the most enriching experiences of my life. I'd been invited into situations I could never have imagined, and I managed to hold together through it all. I met wonderful people under the most terrible of circumstances and felt a deeper connection to humankind than ever before. I saw more, felt more, and learned more than I had during any experience in my previous fifty-plus years on this earth.

Like many others before me, I found there are no answers to the question of why bad things happen to the most innocent among us. I discovered that being present with others was the best gift I could offer. Even when we stood together in silence, it was not a silence that divided us but one that bound us together in our common humanity. I learned to listen well (or at least better) in order to hear what was being communicated behind and beyond words. I became aware of personal biases and beliefs, the "personal potholes" I needed to navigate around in order to be fully present for others. I grasped that one can only "pastor" out of who they genuinely are, and I believe I did this.

Yet in the end, I discovered that the role of chaplain was not, for me, the natural extension beyond playing music I had hoped it would be. These two callings represented vastly different experiences in terms of expectations and demands.

As a chaplain, I wore a tie and carried the Bible. As a musician, I wore a brightly colored shirt and carried a guitar.

As a chaplain, I was expected to use "God" language. As a musician, I was directed to avoid songs containing overtly religious messages.

Most families felt they could not say "no" to a visit from a chaplain, yet a "no" to my offer of a song occurred regularly and was viewed positively.

As a chaplain, there was time to explore families' needs. As a musician, I needed to quickly assess the situation, select and perform a song, and depart.

The contrast between the two roles was best exemplified by two separate exchanges I had with nurses during the same week. In the first case, I performed the role of chaplain in the emergency department following a trauma. After extensive and unsuccessful attempts to save a child, as staff began to exit the critical care unit, one of the nurses stopped to look at me and said, "You have the toughest job in the hospital."

Later that week, while I was serving in the role of musician, a nurse commented, "You have the easiest job in the hospital."

Looking ahead, I expected to resume playing for children at some point, though I wasn't sure when. Thanks to my chaplaincy experience, I would no doubt find it easier to approach the doors of strangers and enter their lives for a few moments with music. I could see now how a single song might provide an invitation to a deeper discussion, and I would be on the lookout for those situations in which music opened the opportunity for such a talk.

Although I stayed away from the hospital for months following my CPE experience, the emotional connection I felt to that world and to the people who work and suffer inside those walls remained intact. Each time I passed the exit I had taken on my drive to the hospital, I recalled the people I'd met, their faces and stories preserved in my memory. When a CareFlite helicopter flew overhead in that direction, I offered a silent prayer that the staff and chaplains waiting for it to arrive would be given the strength, healing, and wisdom they needed.

Despite my residual emotional connection, I avoided returning to the hospital for eight months. This self-imposed moratorium might have continued much longer had I not received an invitation that was perfectly framed from a source I could not refuse.

# Chapter Nineteen
## Butterfly Bubbles

Today at the hospital...

...I had the pleasant experience of pulling into the lot designated primarily for visitor and volunteer parking and discovering that after eight months away, my volunteer badge still allowed me free parking privileges. I took this as a good sign of things to come.

I started the long trek toward the hospital, guitar case in hand. In the past, when I'd come here to play, I'd enjoyed passing through the enclosed walkway connecting the parking structure to the hospital. The many large windows on both sides always allowed abundant natural light to brighten the hallway and, by extension, my attitude. But during my time as chaplain, this space had felt like a transition zone where I could take one last deep breath before plunging into the deep end. Perhaps aided by the passing of time, today it felt more welcoming.

Just beyond the main desk, I stopped at a bank of windows to look down at one of the hospital's more unique exhibits. On the level below, toy trains carved their way through model build-ings that mimicked a downtown skyline. I noticed the schedule posted at the eye level of a child and was pleased to see the trains were running on time. A boy tethered to an IV pole smiled with excitement as he identified for his father the numerous action figures posing on streets and hanging from fake buildings. I had walked past this positive space that captures imaginations hundreds of times before today. Somehow, until now, I had never taken it in. It was as though I was seeing the hospital again for the first time.

I had returned to the hospital for my first visit in well over two hundred days because the invitation to provide music for today's service was impossible to refuse. For a small handful of people, my operating principle is to perform anything they request, no questions asked, and Laura is one of those people. After the exceptionally difficult night on call chronicled in "Recorded in Red" in Part Three of this book, she was the chaplain waiting in the office to settle, center, and comfort me. When she asked if I would provide the music for the remem-brance service coordinated by the pastoral care office to honor the memory of children who had died during the past eighteen months, I could not say no.

As I picked up my guitar to continue my trek to the audi-torium where the service was to be held, I caught my reflection in the windowpane in front of me. Dressed in a coat and tie, I looked every bit the part of a chaplain, but today I was carrying the tools of the musician trade.

I had never seen this combined image before because I had never allowed these two worlds to meld. Despite the encouragement of my peers to incorporate music into my work as chaplain, I had stubbornly resolved to keep these two ways of serving separate.

"I don't want to force the connection," I'd told them. "I want to learn a new role and acquire a new set of tools."

But eight months after my chaplaincy ended, I doubted the wisdom of that stance. Thanks to Laura, the two roles had now been invited to come together in a way I had intentionally avoided.

Rows of chairs were neatly organized when I arrived at the auditorium, a circular multi-purpose room that serves as the site for everything from flu shots to training sessions to memorial services like this one.

An array of small white vials sprawled atop the tables on both sides of the entrance immediately caught my attention. As I stopped to take a closer look, I noticed the plastic shape of a small butterfly perched on the cap of each bottle. A small piece of paper with the first name of every child who had been a patient here and died during the past year and a half was tied around the neck of each vial. There were too many to count.

The service began with a welcome from the head of the pastoral care department. The audience of employees and medical staff was smaller than I'd expected, given the number of seats available. Because only a few medical staff came, the audience was comprised mostly of hospital management. I admired their presence.

Following the introductory comments, I sang and played a song titled "Coming Home." I chose it because the lyrics and descending chord progressions felt appropriate for the solemn occasion. When I sang the second verse, the words Jim Newton wrote for a friend's house-blessing ceremony seemed to fit this hospital setting:

> *So celebrate together*
>
> *Comfort all who come*
>
> *Family, friends, and loved ones*
>
> *We are coming home*
>
> *Together once again*
>
> *Feels so warm and good*
>
> *Family and friends*
>
> *We are coming home*
>
> *Safe within these walls*
>
> *Peaceful place to rest*
>
> *Welcome one and all*
>
> *We are coming home*

I had practiced the song many times at home, but as I sang it here in the hospital, I found reassurance in the words. I suddenly felt "safe within these walls." Once again, I felt welcomed here. For the first time in a long time, it felt "warm and good" to be among a group of chaplains who were pursuing the critical care-giving work I felt unequipped to continue, seeking to "comfort all who come."

When I finished the song, a team of chaplains took turns reading aloud the names of each deceased child, twenty names at a time.

Minutes passed. The list seemed endless. Eventually, I heard the names "Marcus" and "Daniel," two boys who had arrived at the hospital on my watch. I found it curious how my memories of these events had both focused and faded. I recalled their cases and the faces of their families as if it were yesterday, yet for some reason it all seemed to have happened a very long time ago.

The service concluded with an invitation from Laura to explore the vials on the tables. She told us they were filled with bubbles that were ethereal and floating, fragile and beautiful, and that the butterfly on the top of each cap symbolized the shortness of each child's life. She said, "Each name represents a child who died this past eighteen months. Please feel free to read the names and choose those you would like to honor. As you carry these bubbles with you, whenever you blow them, hold the memory of that special child with you."

At first, I considered her suggestion to take the vials with Marcus' and Daniel's names rather pointless. After all, I had carried the memory of these boys with me for the past eight months. But I discovered that taking the vials offered a new, albeit delayed, sense of closure to my chaplaincy. I guess a lot of things seem silly or meaningless until you try them.

It was only through chance that I was on call the nights those boys arrived and was given the gift of spending time with their families. I never had the opportunity to get to know either child. I never even said hello to them. Worse, their families never had the chance to bid them good-bye as they would have wanted.

I once heard a wise chaplain say, "No parent is ready for the death of their child, no matter how sick that child may be." That statement resonates with me, coming as close to an absolute truth as can be uttered. I still cannot fathom how painful such loss must be. Today's service in which over three hundred names were read aloud offered testimony to the harsh reality that thousands of children die in our hospitals each year, leaving families to grieve over what might have been.

In the English language, someone who has lost their spouse is called a widow or widower. Children who lose their parents are orphans. But to my knowledge, there is no word in our language for a parent who loses a child. That is how it should be, I think. Recognition that there are no words, much less a single word, that can adequately capture the pain of that loss.

As I made the long walk back to my car after the service, I questioned why I had stayed away for so long, why I had allowed myself to get stuck in the past. I had wanted the chaplain experience to inform my volunteer work as a musician, but for the past eight months, I had let it overwhelm it.

Today's visit to the hospital was indeed a good one. The service was titled "Time to Remember," but for me, it served as a nudge, telling me it was time to move on by coming back to this place, and to bring my music with me.

# Chapter Twenty
## The Boy Next Door

Today at the hospital...

...I completed a song for a little girl and her mother, said my good-byes, and left their room. I was walking down the hallway toward my next assignment when I heard a shout.

"Wait! Wait!"

I turned to see the mother I'd just left rushing out of her daughter's room heading in my direction. Her tone was so urgent that I feared something was wrong, although I couldn't imagine what.

"Can I help you?" I asked.

"Yes. There's a little boy in that room."

She pointed to the door I was standing by.

"He doesn't get many visitors. Could you sing a song for him, too? I think he'd like it."

"Of course," I said. "Thank you for the suggestion."

When I first started playing music, I concentrated on the rooms of patients recommended to me by the child life specialists, but lately I was receiving additional requests from families and staff I met while wandering the floors with my guitar. They'd say something like, "Hey, the kiddo in that room might like a song, too." I interpreted their suggestions as a sign of growing acceptance of music among those most closely connected to the emotional needs of children.

I found the boy sitting in his bed, alone in his room as the mother had suggested he might be. He was only three or four years old. The curtains were closed and the television was turned on, its volume low.

I asked if he would like a song, and he nodded.

"Friends of the Family," the first song I'd learned from the Hugworks repertoire, came to mind as an appropriate choice. While this number is a bit more upbeat than I might normally select for a patient who is alone and in the dark, the message fit the situation so well that I couldn't help but give it a try. I sang:

> Ever been some place, so strange and new,
> Didn't know one face, didn't know just what to do?
> I've been there, too. Felt just like you,
> But I met some friends of the family,
> Friends among the best I've ever known.

When I finished the song, the little boy smiled at me. I bid him farewell and added, "Don't worry. You have neighbors looking out for you here." I hated to leave him all alone, but I had many other rooms to visit.

The hospitalization of a child disrupts family patterns, but I usually find at least one parent or grandparent with each child. Nonetheless, in some families, work responsibilities, sibling schedules, or simply the lack of a strong support system prevent anyone from spending much time at the hospital. I had no idea why this small boy was here all alone, but it saddened me just the same.

A surprising aspect of life in a children's hospital is the way communities of caring develop on the floors. People with vastly different backgrounds come together as neighbors, and a strong sense of fellowship develops as they look out for one another. Today, this special connection in this "home away from home" served as the inspiration behind a song played for one small boy sitting all alone in his hospital room.

I was happy to witness the power of this community in the thoughtful kindness of a mother who, observing the absence of visitors and sensing how lonely the boy must be, went out of her way to help. The mom and the little boy might have been strangers, but she certainly acted like a "friend of the family... among the best I've ever known."

# Chapter Twenty-One
## A Song of Silence

Today at the hospital...

...I had the pleasure of playing for an eight-year-old girl and her parents. When I entered her room, the child was lying in bed, cradled in her mother's arms. I asked if she would like a song, and she nodded ever so slightly. I sensed she was not coming out of sleep but was headed toward it, so I chose "Cotton Candy Clouds," Jim Newton's beautiful lullaby written for his daughters.

When I started to sing the first verse, the little girl's eyes closed. I continued to strum my guitar and softly sing words that felt like they were written for this girl and this moment:

*Cotton candy clouds*

*Rocking chair moon*

*Drifting off to Dreamland*

*Safe here in your room*

*If I could I'd surely*

*Make them all come true*

*All the finest dreams for you*

The mother stroked her daughter's arm while I continued to play. By the time I reached the final verse, the little girl lay in perfect stillness, having fallen into a deep and hopefully long and restful sleep. Her mother whispered her gratitude as I exited the room.

I consider every hospital room visit an honor. I experience the privilege of being welcomed into a place where pain and fear are real. Sometimes there is little in the way of a visual response to the music I provide. I leave those rooms with a prayer that some good came out of the visit. But more often than not, sometimes in unexpected ways, a special sense of purpose flows back to me from those I serve. Today was a day like that, even if the response came in the form of silence, thanks to a peacefully sleeping child.

French composer Claude Debussy is credited with saying, "Music is the space between the notes."

The healing power of music sometimes becomes evident in a similar manner, in the silence that follows a song.

# Chapter Twenty-Two
## Taking a Shot

Today at the hospital...

...I could hear the screams of the young child from the hallway, even with the closed door blocking the space between us.

I stood outside the door, pausing to study the patient census, hoping I might have the wrong room.

No such luck. I knocked on the door, opened it, and peered inside at a mother holding a boy between eighteen and twenty-four months in her arms.

To say he was upset would be a vast understatement. Still screaming, he took uncontrollable hitched breaths as tears streamed down his face.

I asked if I could offer a little music as a way to help out, and the mother nodded.

A nurse stood next to them, trying to give the child a shot. I sensed her frustration as she glanced at my guitar and whispered in a low voice, "Good luck."

There aren't many songs that come to mind in a situation like this. The best approach when a child is this upset is to select something quiet and soothing that might diminish the tension, but there are no guarantees.

I've also learned it's wise to have an exit strategy in mind before you begin. If the song didn't help, I'd continue playing while slowly backing out of the room. This solution would honor the feedback the child was providing without abandoning my belief that the music, if given sufficient time, would ultimately be helpful.

I started playing a quiet ballad. The child, still shaking and sobbing, quickly took note. He seemed intrigued by my guitar and my presence, likely in that order. His head alternated between burrowing in his mother's shoulder and peering over it to find the source of the music.

At the height of his distraction, the nurse made her move. She inserted the needle in his slender arm, and he never felt it pierce his skin. He kept looking at me and my guitar, trying to make sense of this sonic curiosity.

By the time I finished the song, the room was peaceful. The music had served as a non-invasive way to distract this little boy and alleviate his anxiety. Stated more simply, I had taken my shot, and the little boy had taken his.

I thanked the mother and son and left, feeling relief and appreciation that this room had been on my list. As I turned to leave, the nurse asked, "Can you come with me to see all my patients?" I smiled and told her I wished I could.

Extreme cases like this remind me of how versatile music is. It has the potential to energize us, calm us, and everything in between. What an extraordinary healing tool.

# Chapter Twenty-Three
## Bookends

Today at the hospital...

...There needed to be two, maybe three, maybe even more of us. The demand for music outstripped my capacity to provide it.

That today would be busier than normal became clear as soon as I entered the front door. Passing by the admitting waiting area on my way to the volunteer office, I noticed a young girl in a small pediatric wheelchair. As I passed, one of the women sitting next to her made a comment about my guitar, and I smiled.

A couple of minutes later, after tuning my guitar and picking up the longer-than-normal list of patients to visit, I headed off to the individual rooms. As I walked back through the waiting area, I heard the woman make another, more audible, comment, so I turned and asked if they'd like a song.

The little girl, perhaps six or seven, was looking at an iPad. I sat down on one of the large round coffee tables near her so we could be at the same eye level. When I started to play a song, she set the tablet on her lap and pulled herself closer to me.

Face to face, I could see that she was a child with special needs. She smiled and watched as I fingered the chords, occasionally glancing at the adults behind me. When I finished the song, she smiled brightly. I wished her a good day and started toward the elevator, glad for the opportunity to start my rounds this way.

The rest of my day continued in this vein, with impromptu requests for music surprising me at almost every turn. On the first floor I visited, a mother who heard my music emerged from a room and asked if I could play for her son.

During an elevator ride between floors, one staff member told me she personally could use a song. I strummed a couple of chords for her and exited the elevator to her encouraging words, "Go make a kid happy."

As I walked toward the next room on my list, a nurse called out, "This little guy could use a song."

I turned around and saw a boy of about two perched on her lap at the nurses' station. There were bruises around his face, particularly under his left eye. The fact that he was sitting with nurses at their work station suggested he might not be receiving much company. The oddly straightforward and non-technical diagnosis of "multiple bruises" on his census form suggested that someone close to him had done something to cause him to be admitted.

I hunched down to get closer to his level as I began to sing "If I Had a Truck." This is a song that tends to work nicely with the youngest of children since it uses a truck as a playful metaphor about delivering payloads of love.

*Truck, truck, if I had a truck*

*Truck, truck, if I had a truck*

*If I had a truck I'd fill it up with love and come along and dump on you*

*The biggest hug in town*

*I'd put my arms around*

*And maybe you would squeeze me, too.*

I sang all three verses to the song, but the little boy offered no response. He stared at my guitar but rarely made eye contact with me, taking in the music while remaining distant and detached. It was clear he needed far more than a truckload of love and a single song from a stranger to make the physical and emotional pain he was experiencing go away.

After a half dozen more room visits, I was done for the day, but the contrasting images of the responsive girl in the waiting room and the sad little boy on the nurse's lap remained with me well into the evening. Their responses bookend what it's like to provide music to children in the hospital.

Today, I left feeling unable to do enough but grateful I'd had the opportunity to try. The need was so great that I couldn't get to everyone who might have benefited from a song. Meanwhile, one boy's pain was so deep that the music simply couldn't reach him.

# Chapter Twenty-Four
## My Little Translator

Today at the hospital...

...There weren't many children on the list provided to me, and most were either sleeping or away from their rooms when I stopped by. On days like this, it might be easy to wonder if the trip is worth the effort, but I've learned not to think in those terms. You never know when the next room will be the most important stop of the day.

The last room on my list was on the oncology floor. The census form indicated the patient was a Spanish-speaking fifteen-month-old female, which struck me as far too young to have cancer. As I peeked through the window, I could see a fairly large group of visitors. I knocked, entered, and asked if the little girl would like a song. The response from the crowd was enthusiastic.

I introduced myself to the five adult women I assumed were the mother, grandmother, and some combination of aunts or friends. The little girl was facing away from me while seated on the lap of her mother. The back of her head revealed a semi-circular track of a surgical scar that covered her entire crown. Even though she was awake, I said I would play something soft and soothing.

The mother turned the child to face me. Older scars populated her face and head, providing evidence of earlier surgeries. I tried not to think about the suffering she had endured at such a young age.

I started playing John Denver's ballad, "For Baby." I have found it to be a go-to song in situations like this one because it contains a soothing melody and meaningful lyrics, a combination that speaks to children and adults alike.

When I started to sing, the little girl pushed herself off her mother's lap and stood up. Now able to see me more clearly, she smiled and jumped as if to dance. The grandmother, now standing by my side, laughed and said, "Baila."

"Dancing," I replied. She nodded, and we smiled at each other.

By now the smart phones were out, recording a combination of my singing and the little one's response. I looked toward the row of adults seated on the far side of the bed. One woman was wiping tears from her eyes. A Bible sat open on her lap.

I started the second verse, and in the middle of the line the child loudly smacked her lips, to which the grandmother said, "Beso."

I echoed with "Kiss." She was translating her granddaughter's actions into her language, and I was translating her words into mine.

At that moment, it dawned on me what was happening. The next line in the song contained that same word. I knew it wasn't possible, but it seemed as though this tiny girl, too young to speak, was somehow acting out the lyrics to the song even before I sang them, thanking the adults who surrounded her for their love. The visible scars and the pain that must have come with them had not dimmed this child's bright and shining inner spirit.

There is power in a single song. Music is a universal language with the potential to unite us in our common humanity. I know that not all of my words were understood in that room, but they didn't need to be. I had my own little translator acting out the song's message of unconditional love.

I bade them all farewell, gave the child a smile, and walked out the room. It was only one visit, but it was a perfect visit. Next week, I'll come back for more.

# Chapter Twenty-Five
## Common Ground at Last

Today at the hospital...

...I stood at the foot of the bed of a two-year-old girl who was undergoing what can only be called a miraculous recovery. Next to me stood her father, his guitar in hand, and together we played and joyously sang "This Little Light of Mine."

I first met the father three months ago, after offering a song to another child. He was seated in the hallway with two other men, and when I paused to look over my census, he commented on my guitar, asking, "So you do music here?"

I shared with him the concept of "musical hugs," and he smiled at the description. Our conversation then turned to guitars, our favorite songs, and our preferred musical genres, particularly bluegrass and gospel.

Then, quite abruptly, his face turned serious. "My daughter Angie is in the ICU, in a coma," he said. "She's in pretty bad shape. It's a miracle she even survived the accident. Maybe you could look for her next time you're here."

I asked how he and his family were coping in this hospital in a city many miles from home, and he exuded a cautious optimism in his reply.

"We're all taking it one day at a time. Here's our picture with our contact information written on the back. Please pray for us."

Each time I returned to the hospital over the next several months, I asked the child life specialists for Angie's room number, and each visit was much like the first one. Her father and I would visit for a few minutes, and then he would grab his guitar and we would play a song while Angie lay motionless with a myriad of tubes and monitor wires running from her body to the Extracorporeal Membrane Oxygenation (ECMO) equipment stationed beside her bed. Reserved for the very sick, ECMO equipment handles the workload of managing lung and heart functions, providing bodies the time they need to rest and heal.

Despite the uncertain prognosis that accompanies this treatment, each member of Angie's family continuously displayed a quiet confidence, grounded in an inner faith that was apparent in every word and expression.

Privately, my pessimistic side worried they might be expecting too much both from medical technology and from God. After all, Angie was entering her fourth month as a patient here.

One day, I arrived at the ICU to find a sign posted on the door to her room that read, "Please check with nurse before entering."

Uncertain of the real meaning behind these words, I pressed my face to the glass and peered inside, but there was no one in sight. When I spotted Angie's pink blanket strewn along the edge of the bed, I feared the worst.

I hurried to the nurse's station only a few feet away and asked, "Can you tell me where the family in that room might be? I've visited them a couple of times, and I just want to know if everything is okay."

"They're in the room now," the nurse replied very matter-of-factly. "Didn't you see them? They're sitting on the floor."

I shot back to the door, knocked quietly, and entered. On the far side of the bed, I found Angie sitting on the floor, her mother and grandmother on each side of her.

My heart leaped. Angie was awake, alert, sitting up on her own, breathing, playing, responding, experiencing, living! I sang a short song for her and then exited to avoid intruding on the family's precious multi-generational playtime.

The next week when I returned to the ICU, I was surprised to find a teenage girl occupying the room. I ran down to the hospital's child life office and asked where Angie and her family might be and was directed to the rehabilitation unit on a different floor.

When I entered the room, I found Angie sleeping. Her father greeted me and we sat together as he shared the good news of his daughter's amazing progress.

Then he reached behind me and grabbed his guitar, which was standing in the corner. "Let's play some music," he suggested.

I taught him a Hugworks song, and in return he shared his engaging arrangement of a gospel favorite. Noticing his daughter stirring a bit, we positioned ourselves at the foot of her bed. As Angie awakened, her eyes widened and brightened at the sight of the two of us.

"Let's play 'This Little Light of Mine' in the key of G," Angie's father said to me before leaning in closer to his daughter.

"Where's your light?" he asked her, and she pointed her index finger to the ceiling, referencing a much higher plane, the heavens above.

With each verse, Angie became more and more engaged. When we sang "Hide it under a bushel?", she immediately responded, "No!"

When we warned of Satan, she quickly exhaled toward her raised index finger and voiced, "Phew."

I watched in awe as this two-year-old who had so recently emerged from a coma blossomed like a springtime flower. Her recovery was a miracle that had taken its sweet time to arrive, perhaps making its appearance all the more joyous.

Later, I reflected on Angie's recovery and my initial encounter with her father. It was music that opened the door to a casual conversation that revealed his reason for being in the hospital. Over the next few months, music provided us with a common ground that deepened as we talked, played, and sang.

But beyond this initial connection, it was my experience as a chaplain that bestowed on me the grace to ask how he was coping and to look for the family each time I returned to the hospital. Had I not served as chaplain, I might not have responded to his opening and would have missed the opportunity to witness and in some small way contribute to this family's amazing journey of faith, strength, and resilience.

My experience today at the hospital offered new insight into the caregiving relationship. Simply put, I became aware that I cared for and about Angie and her family in a more appropriate, more restrained, and more helpful fashion than I cared for Jason and his family.

This realization makes me wonder if the key to serving others has less to do with observing a boundary that separates *caring* from *caring too much* and more to do with finding a sweet spot where I am able to feel and attend to another's pain without staggering under its weight. In this sense, caregiving is like extending a hand to someone who has stumbled and fallen.

Not joining them in the depths of their despair but meeting them halfway by reaching out and lifting them up.

Perhaps I will see Angie and her father again next week when I return and we will share another song together. Or perhaps they will have gone home, for which I will rejoice. Regardless, the song Angie's father and I sang today seems like a proper benediction to a relationship that revealed I am at my best when I allow my chaplain experience to inform and complement my work as therapeutic musician.

# Conclusion
## One Song at a Time

On a number of occasions over the past few years, Jim Newton has introduced me to his Hugworks associates by saying, "Larry used to be a corporate executive."

I cringed inside every time I heard him say this. For reasons I could not articulate, my corporate background and the "executive" label felt like an old coat that no longer fit. One day, I told Jim I would prefer he talk about my work as a therapeutic musician when he introduced me.

There were certainly times during my career when how I viewed myself was tightly woven into external signs of success like job title, office space, and salary. Now I view my work history as something that molded me into who I am today rather than as something that defines me. I am not my résumé.

What defines success in life? The thousands of books written on this topic suggest that anyone willing to master (depending on the guru) the critical steps, the principles, the habits, the attitudes, and/or the laws articulated within can achieve the success they seek. But what defines success is an individual matter as unique as our DNA. How a single set of principles can be so absolute and universal that they work for everyone is beyond my understanding.

Being "plutoed" late in my career launched me on a reluctant but ultimately positive journey I never could have imagined. It took longer than it should have to let go of perceived slights, but eventually I learned that I could not define success as my career wound down in the same way I had defined it during my years on the job.

Somewhere along the way, I found the wisdom to move on. Despite all the noise inside my head about a career cut short and my devalued sense of self-worth, I latched onto something I was good at and love to do – play music. I proceeded with no clear idea where this might take me; I simply trusted it might be somewhere fresh and interesting. In the end, music pulled me like a tractor beam toward a life defined more by service than success, more about self-worth than net worth.

Still, one of life's questions I've continued to find elusive is, "If we are called in our lives to serve others, how do we discern what form that service should take?" If you have read this far, I assume the desire to understand how best to serve is as real for you as it remains for me. Some wait for a voice to tell them in what direction to head. But I wonder if that places too much burden on a busy God and overlooks our personal responsibility to resolve such questions on our own, or at least initiate the process. Perhaps instead of waiting for an answer, we are charged to act and look for signs, both within and outside ourselves, that inform whether we are on the right path.

Because the answer is different for each of us, the path to discernment may be closer to how religious thinker Barbara Brown Taylor described it in her book, *An Altar in the World*: "Wisdom is not gained by *knowing* what is right. Wisdom is gained by *practicing* what is right, and noticing what happens when that practice succeeds and when it fails."

In short, doing leads to discernment.

My journey went something like this: I started with something I truly enjoyed doing. I opened myself to suggestions regarding places where my skills and passion dovetailed with a need. I put these ideas into practice, paying close attention to how others responded and how this experience felt for me. I pushed the experience to what seemed like the next logical step, trusting that these new experiences would produce meaning and inform new directions. I explored foreign boundaries that exposed my personal limits. I came to understand what I was capable of and, more importantly, what I could not do. Eventually, experience pointed me back to a sweet spot where my passion intersected with a real human need, a place where I was content staying true to the essential me, where life was no longer defined by what I did for a living but by what I did for others.

This kind of "try and adjust" approach may be too loose and unstructured to work within the "keys to success" frameworks that permeate corporate life because it values process over achieving results against measurable objectives. It emphasizes taking risks versus making decisions based on research and data, values vulnerability over power, and seeks to help others as equals instead of controlling them as subordinates. Spending half a lifetime in business did little to prepare me for the life that followed my career because the principles I learned in the corporate world didn't apply.

I found that acting in a caring manner was the first step toward becoming a more compassionate person. Having grown up on a farm, an agricultural metaphor works for me. We must plow the earth of our souls until it is no longer rocky ground. In so doing, we open ourselves toward an understanding of how we can use our unique talents in a more intentional way, employing the seeds of service already planted within us.

This notion reverses our typical view of things. We tend to embrace the concept that beliefs lead to behaviors. For example, I must believe I will like a movie before I go see it or believe I will enjoy a new restaurant before I visit it. But through service to others, I discovered the opposite flow works as well, perhaps better. Placing myself in situations where the needs of others, not my own, were paramount led me to become more focused on others. It was my actions that changed my beliefs regarding what I needed to do, not the other way around.

I recall high-level discussions during my business career about building a positive corporate culture. The concept of "working culture" felt too vague to wrap my head around. "I don't understand how something so amorphous can impact how we work together and make decisions," I said. But a colleague suggested it worked in the opposite direction, that our "culture" was the cumulative result of each and every action we took, no matter how big or small. In a similar way, our beliefs do not merely guide our actions but are revealed through what we do.

I find myself wondering and imagining what next avenue I should pursue, something that will send me in directions I might not embrace if I knew them in advance. There is something simultaneously appealing and scary in taking a first step, in making the initial move into uncharted territory where I will encounter new demands that require me to adapt and grow.

For now, I will return to the hospital each week and play music for children and their family members. It's not as difficult for me as it once was, although it's not easy, nor perhaps should it ever be. I walk into situations where I know the music can only do so much, fully aware that it's not enough. The stakes are high, and I know I need to elevate myself and my game to meet the challenge. But I draw great comfort in knowing this is something I can do in service of others.

On some days, the response is not very evident, but I no longer consider that a failure because "failure" reflects the language of the business world. On my best days, I get a front row seat to watch the amazing power of music to make life better, if only for a few minutes, in a place where children suffer and parents worry.

I am confident today that I could answer my friend Richard's questions about the enduring value of music, about why I sing songs, and why they matter. If asked, I would tell him stories about what I have witnessed while singing songs to severely ill children and their families. I would describe images of tears shed and laughter shared. I would tell him about exuberant dancing and how I feel when I am able to distract a child from pain and boredom and fear. These responses are mental works of art painted on the canvas of my memory, ready for me to view any time I wish.

That is why I have shared these stories. I hope that by putting them into words, others will gain a picture of what I have witnessed – the enormous power of a single song.

I will continue to return to the hospital, looking forward to the next child I meet and the song I will provide. In the hospital, my music matters, and so do I. I succeed through service.

Providing music for severely ill children is not some bold act designed to attract attention or change the world. I will leave expansive missions like that to leaders more capable than I am. Instead, I am content in the knowledge that the act of showing up, of providing a "musical hug," tells these hospitalized children they matter. I hope this small act speaks volumes, letting them know that if a stranger cares enough to show up, countless others must be rooting for them as well.

Today at the hospital, I will approach a child's room and adjust the blinds on the door window to see if it might be a good time for a visit. I will knock on the door and introduce myself without status or title. "Hello. I'm Larry. The folks from child life suggested I stop by to see if you would like a song."

I will be satisfied with whatever happens next, whether it's acceptance or rejection. But deep inside, I hope each child will say, "Yes," because it means there is a chance the magic moment will occur when the power of a single song collides with an emotional need and it changes a small slice of this world for the better.

# Author Biography

Larry Dykstra is a first-time author who discovered that as his business career ended, he had much more to learn.

In 2010, Larry began a journey to broaden his focus and rebalance his life's priorities. Curious by nature and a lifelong intentional learner, he pursued a number of experiences that introduced him to new worlds and stretched him as a person. These experiences explored three broad and relevant themes: playing music with and for others, serving hospitalized children, and exploring matters of spirituality and healing.

Over the next six years, Larry spent more than six hundred hours in children's hospitals as a therapeutic music entertainer and as a chaplain in the pastoral care department. In the process, he discovered that he could no longer define success by what he did for a living but by what he did for others.

A self-taught musician, Larry has the gifted ability to lead informal sing-alongs that engage audiences. He is currently a member of multiple ensembles playing music genres ranging from R&B, acoustic rock, and worship. Depending on the group, song, and audience, Larry handles a combination of rhythm guitar, mandolin, and lead or back-up vocals.

As a speaker at professional research and marketing conferences and corporate events, Larry has produced original viewpoints on business-relevant topics such as the consumer insight discipline, innovation, group decision-making, and communication.

Leveraging his work experience, Larry remains connected to the business world by providing strategic planning, consumer insight, and new product innovation services for numerous well-known companies as a consultant partner for Flight3 Marketing.

Larry currently resides in Dallas, Texas and has been married to his best friend Sandy for thirty-five years. "Taco Tuesday" family dinners with Sandy, their sons Charlie and Evan, Charlie's wife Molly, and their two grandchildren Emerson and Owen are his favorite part of each week.

# An Invitation

For most of my life, music was merely a source of entertainment, something I loved that made life more enjoyable. In time, I began to marvel at the emotional impact it had on vastly different audiences in a wide range of contexts.

Nowhere was the boundless power of music more apparent than when I sang at the bed-sides of children in hospitals. I came to call these expressions of caring offered in the form of a song "musical hugs." I found my experiences so compelling I began writing about what it looked and felt like to bring the gift of live music to the most vulnerable of audiences. This book is the result of that effort.

My continuing interest as a writer is to share personal stories that reveal music in action. I can easily imagine "musical hugs" are happening all around us each and every day, so I invite you to share your personal stories of how music has touched your life or that of someone you know. My hope is that together we can build a greater appreciation for the countless ways music intersects with emotional needs and makes a positive difference.

Please share your "musical hug" story, as either giver or receiver, with me at musicalhugs.com.

I look forward to hearing from you!